On the *Revival of the Religious Sciences* (*Iḥyāʾ ʿulūm al-dīn*)

"The *Iḥyāʾ ʿulūm al-dīn* is the most valuable and most beautiful of books."

—Ibn Khallikān (d. 681/1282)

"The *Iḥyāʾ ʿulūm al-dīn* is one of al-Ghazālī's best works."

—Aḥmad b. ʿAbd al-Ḥalīm (d. 728/1328)

"Any seeker of [felicity of] the hereafter cannot do without the *Iḥyāʾ ʿulūm al-dīn*"

—Tāj al-Dīn al-Subkī (d. 771/1370)

"The *Iḥyāʾ ʿulūm al-dīn* is a marvelous book containing a wide variety of Islamic sciences intermixed with many subtle accounts of Sufism and matters of the heart."

—Ibn Kathīr (d. 774/1373)

"The *Iḥyāʾ ʿulūm al-dīn* is one of best and greatest books on admonition, it was said concerning it, 'if all the books of Islam were lost except for the *Iḥyāʾ* it would suffice what was lost.'"

—Ḥājjī Khalīfa Katib Čelebī (d. 1067/1657)

"The *Iḥyāʾ* [*ʿulūm al-dīn*] is one of [Imām al-Ghazālī's] most noble works, his most famous work, and by far his greatest work'"

—Muḥammad Murtaḍā l-Zabīdī (d. 1205/1791)

On Imām al-Ghazālī

"Al-Ghazālī is [like] a deep ocean [of knowledge]."

—Imām al-Ḥaramayn al-Juwaynī (d. 478/1085)

"Al-Ghazālī is the second [Imām] Shāfiʿī."

—Muḥammad b. Yaḥyā l-Janzī (d. 549/1154)

"Abū Ḥāmid al-Ghazālī, the Proof of Islam (Ḥujjat al-Islām) and the Muslims, the Imām of the *imāms* of religion, [is a man] whose like eyes have not seen in eloquence and elucidation, and speech and thought, and acumen and natural ability."

—ʿAbd al-Ghāfir b. Ismāʿīl al-Fārisī (d. 529/1134)

"[He was] the Proof of Islam and Muslims, Imām of the imāms of religious sciences, one of vast knowledge, the wonder of the ages, the author of many works, and [a man] of extreme intelligence and the best of the sincere."

—Imām al-Dhahabī (d. 748/1347)

"Al-Ghazālī is without doubt the most remarkable figure in all Islam."

—T.J. DeBoer

". . . A man who stands on a level with Augustine and Luther in religious insight and intellectual vigor."

—H.A.R. Gibb

"I have to some extent found, and I believe others can find, in the words and example of al-Ghazālī a true *iḥyāʾ* . . ."

—Richard J. McCarthy, S.J.

وَمَن يُوقَ شُحَّ نَفْسِهِۦ فَأُو۟لَـٰٓئِكَ هُمُ ٱلْمُفْلِحُونَ ١٦

And whoever is protected from the stinginess of his soul -
it is those who will be the successful.

Sūrat al-Taghabun 64:16

The Forty Books of the Revival of the Religious Sciences (*Iḥyāʾ ʿulūm al-dīn*)

The Quarter of Worship

1 The Book of Knowledge
2 The Principles of the Creed
3 The Mysteries of Purification
4 The Mysteries of the Prayer
5 The Mysteries of Charity
6 The Mysteries of Fasting
7 The Mysteries of the Pilgrimage
8 The Etiquette of the Recitation of the Qurʾān
9 Invocations and Supplications
10 The Arrangement of the Litanies and the Exposition of the Night Vigil

The Quarter of Customs

11 The Proprieties of Eating
12 The Proprieties of Marriage
13 The Proprieties of Acquisition and Earning a Living
14 The Lawful and the Unlawful
15 The Proprieties of Friendship and Brotherhood
16 The Proprieties of Retreat
17 The Proprieties of Travel
18 The Proprieties of the Audition and Ecstasy
19 The Commanding of Right and the Forbidding of Wrong
20 The Proprieties of Living and the Prophetic Mannerisms

The Quarter of Perils

21 The Exposition of the Wonders of the Heart
22 Training the Soul, Refining the Character, and Treating the Ailments of the Heart
23 Overcoming the Two Desires
24 The Banes of the Tongue
25 The Banes of Anger, Malice, and Envy
26 The Censure of This World
27 **The Censure of Wealth and Miserliness**
28 The Censure of Fame and Hypocritical Ostentation
29 The Censure of Pride and Vanity
30 The Censure of Deceit

The Quarter of Deliverance

31 On Repentance
32 On Patience and Thankfulness
33 On Fear and Hope
34 On Poverty and Abstinence
35 On Unity and Trust
36 On Love, Longing, Intimacy, and Contentment
37 On Intention, Sincerity, and Truthfulness
38 On Vigilance and Accounting
39 On Contemplation
40 On the Remembrance of Death and the Hereafter

THE CENSURE OF WEALTH AND MISERLINESS

Kitāb dhamm al-māl wal-bukhul

Book 27 of

Iḥyāʾ ʿulūm al-dīn

The Revival of the Religious Sciences

بِسۡمِ ٱللَّهِ ٱلرَّحۡمَٰنِ ٱلرَّحِيمِ

AL-GHAZĀLĪ

Kitāb dhamm al-māl wa-l-bukhl

THE CENSURE OF WEALTH AND MISERLINESS

Book 27 of the *Iḥyāʾ ʿulūm al-dīn*

THE REVIVAL OF THE RELIGIOUS SCIENCES

Translated *from the* Arabic

with Notes

by Nancy N. Roberts

Fons Vitae
2024

The Censure of Wealth and Miserliness, Book 27 of
The Revival of the Religious Sciences first published in 2024 by

Fons Vitae
49 Mockingbird Valley Drive
Louisville, KY 40207 USA

www.fonsvitae.com

The Fons Vitae Ghazali Series
Library of Congress Control Number: 2024947950
ISBN 978-1-94-1610-72-5

Ediitor: Elena Lloyd-Sidle
Series editor: Muhammad Hozien
Book design: www.scholarlytype.com
Typesetting: Neville Blakemore, Jr.
Text typeface: Adobe Minion Pro 11/13.5

Cover art courtesy of National Library of Egypt in Cairo.
Qurʾānic frontispiece to part 19. Written and illuminated by ʿAbdallāh
b. Muḥammad al-Ḥamadānī for Sultan Ūljāytū (Muḥammad
Khudābanda Öljeytü) 713/1313. Hamadan.

Printed in Canada

Contents

Editor's Note

This is the complete translation of the *Kitāb dhamm al-māl wa-l-bukhl*, *The Censure of Wealth and Miserliness*, book 27 of the *Iḥyāʾ ʿulūm al-dīn* of Ḥujjat al-Islām, Abū Ḥāmid al-Ghazālī. It was translated from the published Arabic text of volume 6, pp. 113–253 by Dār al-Minhāj of Jedda (2011), which utilized additional manuscripts and early printed editions.

Arabic terms and names follow the transliteration system of the *International Journal of Middle East Studies*. Common era (CE) dates have been added and follow Hijri dates. The blessings on prophets and others, as used by Imām al-Ghazālī, are represented in the original Arabic, as listed below.

Arabic	English	Usage
عَزَّ وَجَلَّ	Mighty and majestic is He	On mention of God
سُبْحَانَهُ وَتَعَالَىٰ	Exalted and most high is He	Used together or separately
صَلَّى ٱللَّهُ عَلَيْهِ وَسَلَّمَ	Blessings and peace of God be upon him	On mention of the Prophet Muḥammad
عَلَيْهِ ٱلسَّلَامُ	Peace be upon him	On mention of one or more prophets
عَلَيْهِمُ ٱلسَّلَامُ	Peace be upon them	
رَضِيَ ٱللَّهُ عَنْهُ	God be pleased with him	On mention of one or more Companions of the Prophet
رَضِيَ ٱللَّهُ عَنْهُمْ	God be pleased with them	
رَضِيَ ٱللَّهُ عَنْهَا	God be pleased with her	On mention of a female Companion of the Prophet
رَحِمَهُ ٱللَّهُ	God have mercy on him	On mention of someone who is deceased

The majority of sources in the notes are from the Dār al-Minhāj editors. Other explanatory information is provided by the translator (preceded by Trans.) and the editor (preceded by Ed.).

In addition, we have compiled a short biography of Imām al-Ghazālī with a chronology of important events in his life. This is followed by an extract from Imām al-Ghazālī's introduction to the *Iḥyāʾ ʿulūm al-dīn;* it serves as a guide to the *Revival of the Religious Sciences* for those reading Imām al-Ghazālī for the first time. For this edition we included the page numbers of this book in volume 5 of the Arabic edition; these appear in the margins.

Biography of Imām al-Ghazālī

He is Abū Ḥāmid Muḥammad b. Muḥammad b. Muḥammad b. Aḥmad al-Ghazālī l-Ṭūsī; he was born in 450/1058 in the village of Ṭābarān near Ṭūs (in northeast Iran) and he died there, at the age of fifty-five, in 505/1111. Muḥammad's father died when he and his younger brother Aḥmad were still young; their father left a little money for their education in the care of a Sufi friend of limited means. When the money ran out, their caretaker suggested that they enroll in a *madrasa*. The *madrasa* system meant they had a stipend, room, and board. Al-Ghazālī studied *fiqh* in his hometown under a Sufi named Aḥmad al-Rādhakānī; he then traveled to Jurjān and studied under Ismāʿīl b. Masʿada al-Ismāʿīlī (d. 477/1084).

On his journey home, his caravan was overtaken by highway robbers who took all of their possessions. Al-Ghazālī went to the leader of the bandits and demanded his notebooks. The leader asked, "What are these notebooks?" Al-Ghazālī answered, "This is the knowledge that I traveled far to acquire." The leader acquiesced to al-Ghazālī's demands after stating, "If you claim that it is knowledge that you have, how can we take it away from you?" This incident left a lasting impression on the young scholar. Thereafter, he returned to Ṭūs for three years, where he committed to memory all that he had learned thus far.

In 469/1077, he traveled to Nīshāpūr to study with the leading scholar of his time, Imām al-Ḥaramayn al-Juwaynī (d. 478/1085), at the Niẓāmiyya College; al-Ghazālī remained his student for approximately eight years, until al-Juwaynī died. Al-Ghazālī was one of his most illustrious students, and al-Juwaynī referred to him as "a deep ocean [of knowledge]." As one of al-Juwaynī's star pupils, al-Ghazālī used to fill in as a substitute lecturer in his teacher's absence. He also tutored his fellow students in the subjects that al-Juwaynī taught at the Niẓāmiyya. Al-Ghazālī wrote his first book, on the founding principles of legal theory (*uṣūl al-fiqh*), while studying with al-Juwaynī.

Very little is known about al-Ghazālī's family, though some biographers mention that he married while in Nīshāpūr; others note that he had married in Ṭūs prior to leaving for Nīshāpūr. Some accounts state that he had five children, a son who died early and four daughters. Accounts also indicate that his mother lived to see her son rise to fame and fortune.

After the death of al-Juwaynī, al-Ghazālī went to the camp (*al-muʿaskar*) of the Saljūq *wazīr* Niẓām al-Mulk (d. 485/1192). He stayed at the camp, which was a gathering place for scholars, and quickly distinguished himself among their illustrious company. Niẓām al-Mulk recognized al-Ghazālī's genius and appointed him professor at the famed Niẓāmiyya College of Baghdād.

Al-Ghazālī left for Baghdād in 484/1091 and stayed there four years—it was a very exciting time to be in the heart of the Islamic empire. At the Niẓāmiyya College he had many students, by some estimates as many as three hundred. In terms of his scholarly output, this was also a prolific period in which he wrote *Maqāṣid al-falāsifa*, *Tahāfut al-falāsifa*, *al-Mustaẓhirī*, and other works.

Al-Ghazālī was well-connected politically and socially; we have evidence that he settled disputes related to the legitimacy of the rule of the ʿAbbāsid caliph, al-Mustaẓhir (r. 487–512/1094–1118) who assumed his role as the caliph when he was just fifteen years old, after the death of his father al-Muqtadī (d. 487/1094). Al-Ghazālī issued a *fatwā* of approval of the appointment of al-Mustaẓhir and was present at the oath-taking ceremony.

In Baghdād, al-Ghazālī underwent a spiritual crisis, during which he was overcome by fear of the punishment of the hellfire. He became convinced that he was destined for the hellfire if he did not change his ways; he feared that he had become too engrossed in worldly affairs, to the detriment of his spiritual being. He began to question his true intentions: was he writing and teaching to serve God, or because he enjoyed the fame and fortune that resulted from his lectures. He experienced much suffering, both inward and outward; one day as he stood before his students to present a lecture, he found himself unable to speak. The physicians were unable to diagnose any physical malady. Al-Ghazālī remained in Baghdād for a time, then left his teaching post for the pilgrimage. He left behind fortune, fame, and influence. He was beloved by his numerous students and had many admirers, including the sultan; he was also envied by many. The presumption is that he left in the manner he did—ostensibly to undertake the pilgrimage—because if he had made public his intentions to leave permanently, those around him would have tried to convince him to remain and the temptation might have been too strong to resist.

After leaving Baghdād, he changed direction and headed toward Damascus; according to his autobiography he disappeared from the intellectual scene for ten years. This does not mean that he did not teach, but that he did not want to return to public life and be paid for teaching. This ten-year period can be divided into two phases. First, he spent two years in the East—in greater Syria and on the pilgrimage. We have evidence that while on his return to Ṭūs he appeared at a Sufi lodge opposite the Niẓāmiyya College in Baghdād. He spent the second phase of the ten-year period (the remaining eight years) in Ṭūs, where he wrote the famed *Iḥyāʾ ʿulūm al-dīn*, a work that was inspired by the change in his outlook that resulted from his spiritual crisis.

When he arrived back in his hometown in 490/1097, he established a school and a Sufi lodge, in order to continue teaching and learning. In 499/1106, Niẓām al-Mulk's son, Fakhr al-Mulk, requested that al-Ghazālī accept a teaching position at his old school, the Niẓāmiyya of Nīshāpūr. He accepted and taught for a time, but left this position in 500/1106 after Fakhr al-Mulk was assassinated by Ismāʿīlīs. He then returned to Ṭūs and divided his time between teaching and worship. He died in 505/1111 and was buried in a cemetery near the citadel of Ṭābarān.

Legacy and Contributions of al-Ghazālī

Al-Ghazālī's two hundred seventy-three works span many disciplines and can be grouped under the following headings.

1. Jurisprudence and legal theory. Al-Ghazālī made foundational contributions to Shāfiʿī jurisprudence; his book *al-Wajīz* is a major handbook that has been used in teaching institutions around the world; many commentaries have been written on it, most notably by Abū l-Qāsim ʿAbd al-Karīm al-Rāfiʿī (d. 623/1226). In legal theory, *al-Mustaṣfa min ʿilm al-uṣūl* is considered one of five foundational texts in the discipline.
2. Logic and philosophy. Al-Ghazālī introduced logic in Islamic terms that jurists could understand and utilize. His works on philosophy include the *Tahāfut al-falāsifa*, which has been studied far beyond the Muslim world and has been the subject of numerous commentaries, discussions, and refutations.
3. Theology, including works on heresiography in refutation of Bāṭinī doctrines. He also expounded on the theory of occasionalism.
4. Ethics and educational theory. The *Mīzān al-ʿamal* and other works such as the *Iḥyāʾ ʿulūm al-dīn* mention a great deal on education.
5. Spirituality and Sufism. His magnum opus, the *Iḥyāʾ ʿulūm al-dīn* is a pioneering work in the field of spirituality, in terms of its organization and its comprehensive scope.
6. Various fields. Al-Ghazālī also wrote shorter works in a variety of disciplines, including his autobiography (*al-Munqidh min al-ḍalāl*), works on Qurʾānic studies (*Jawāhir al-Qurʾān*), and political statecraft (*Naṣiḥat al-mūluk*).

Chronology of al-Ghazālī's Life

450/1058	Birth of al-Ghazālī at Ṭūs
c. 461/1069	Began studies at Ṭūs
c. 465/1073	Traveled to Jurjān to study
466–469/1074–1077	Studied at Ṭūs
469/1077	Studied with al-Jūwaynī at the Niẓāmiyya college in Nīshāpūr
473/1080	al-Ghazālī composed his first book, *al-Mankhūl fi l-uṣūl*
477/1084	Death of al-Fāramdhī, one of al-Ghazālī's teachers
25 Rabīʿ II 478/ 20 August 1085	Death of al-Jūwaynī; al-Ghazālī left Nīshāpūr
Jumāda I 484/ July 1091	Appointed to teach at the Niẓāmiyya college in Baghdād
10 Ramaḍān 485/ 14 October 1092	Niẓām-al-Mulk was assassinated
484–487/1091–1094	Studied philosophy
Muḥarrām 487/ February 1094	Attended the oath-taking of the new caliph, al-Mustaẓhir
487/1094	Finished *Maqāṣid al-falāsifa*
5 Muḥarrām 488/ 21 January 1095	Finished *Tahāfut al-falāsifa*
Rajab 488/ July 1095	Experienced a spiritual crisis
Dhū l-Qaʿda 488/ November 1095	Left Baghdād for Damascus
Dhū l-Qaʿda 489/ November – December 1096	Made pilgrimage and worked on the *Iḥyāʾ ʿulūm al-dīn*
Jumāda II 490/ May 1097	Taught from the *Iḥyāʾ ʿulūm al-dīn* during a brief stop in Baghdād
Rajab 490/June 1097	Seen in Baghdād by Abū Bakr b. al-ʿArabī
Fall 490/1097	Returned to Ṭūs

Dhū l-Ḥijja 490/ November 1097	Established a *madrasa* and a *khānqāh* in Ṭūs
Dhū l-Qaʿda 499/ July 1106	Taught at the Niẓāmiyya college in Nīshāpūr
500/1106	Wrote *al-Munqidh min al-ḍalāl*
500/1106	Returned to Ṭūs
28 Dhū l-Ḥijja 502/ 5 August 1109	Finished *al-Mustaṣfā min ʿilm al-uṣūl*
Jumada I 505/ December 1111	Finished *Iljām al-ʿawām ʿan ʿilm al-kalām*
14 Jumada II 505/ 18 December 1111	Imām al-Ghazālī died in Ṭūs

Eulogies in Verse

Because of him the lame walked briskly,
And the songless through him burst into melody.

On the death of Imām al-Ghazālī, Abū l-Muẓaffar Muḥammad al-Abiwardī said of his loss:

He is gone! and the greatest loss which ever afflicted me,
was that of a man who left no one like him among mankind.

About the *Revival of the Religious Sciences*

THE present work is book 27 of Imām al-Ghazālī's forty-volume masterpiece. Below is an excerpt from al-Ghazālī's introduction that explains the arrangement and purpose of the *Iḥyāʾ ʿulūm al-dīn*.

People have composed books concerning some of these ideas, but this book [the *Iḥyāʾ*] differs from them in five ways, by

1. clarifying what they have obscured and elucidating what they have treated casually;
2. arranging what they scattered and putting in order what they separated;
3. abbreviating what they made lengthy and proving what they reported;
4. omitting what they have repeated; and
5. establishing the truth of certain obscure matters that are difficult to understand and which have not been presented in books at all.

For although all the scholars follow one course, there is no reason one should not proceed independently and bring to light something unknown, paying special attention to something his colleagues have forgotten. Or they are not heedless about calling attention to it, but they neglect to mention it in books. Or they do not overlook it, but something prevents them from exposing it [and making it clear].

So these are the special properties of this book, besides its inclusion of all these various kinds of knowledge.

Two things induced me to arrange this book in four parts. The first and fundamental motive is that this arrangement in establishing what is true and in making it understandable is, as it were, inevitable because the branch of knowledge by which one approaches the hereafter is divided into the knowledge of [proper] conduct and the knowledge of [spiritual] unveiling.

By the knowledge of [spiritual] unveiling I mean knowledge and only knowledge. By the science of [proper] conduct I mean knowledge as well as action in accordance with that knowledge. This work will deal only with the science of [proper] conduct, and not with [spiritual] unveiling, which one is not permitted to record in writing, although it is the ultimate aim of saints and the ultimate aim of the sincere. The science of [proper] conduct is merely a path that leads to unveiling and only through that path did the prophets of God communicate with the people and lead them to Him. Concerning [spiritual] unveiling, the prophets عَلَيْهِمُ السَّلَام spoke only figuratively and briefly through signs and symbols, because they realized the inability of people's minds to comprehend. Therefore, since the scholars are heirs of the prophets, they cannot but follow in their footsteps and emulate their way.

The knowledge of [proper] conduct is divided into (1) outward knowledge, by which I mean knowledge of the senses and (2) inward knowledge, by which I mean knowledge of the functions of the heart.

The physical members either perform acts of prescribed worship, or acts that are in accordance with custom, while the heart, because it is removed from the senses and belongs to the world of dominion, is subject to either praiseworthy or blameworthy [influences]. Therefore it is necessary to divide this branch of knowledge into two parts: outward and inward. The outward part, which is connected to the senses, is subdivided into acts of worship and acts that pertain to custom. The inward part, which is connected to the states of the heart and the characteristics of the soul, is subdivided into blameworthy states and praiseworthy states. So the total makes four divisions of the sciences of the practice of religion.

The second motive [for this division] is that I have noticed the sincere interest of students in jurisprudence, which has become popular among those who do not fear God تَعَالَىٰ but who seek to boast and exploit its influence and prestige in arguments. It [jurisprudence] is also divided into four quarters, and he who follows the style of one who is beloved becomes beloved.

THE CENSURE OF WEALTH AND MISERLINESS

Kitāb dhamm al-māl wa-l-bukhl

Book 27 of

Iḥyāʾ ʿulūm al-dīn

The Revival of the Religious Sciences

Author's Introduction

In the Name of God, the All-Merciful, the All-Compassionate

PRAISE be to God, the One worthy of praise for His extensive sustenance, the remover of difficulty after despair, Who created humankind and extended its sustenance, Who poured out all manner of wealth upon the worlds, and tried them through the vicissitudes of fortune, alternately leading them into hardship and ease, affluence (*al-ghinā*) and poverty (*al-faqr*), ambitious greed (*al-ṭamʿ*) and hopelessness (*al-yaʾs*), fortune (*al-tharwa*) and ruin (*al-iflās*), weakness (*al-ʿajz*) and ability (*al-istaṭāʿa*), covetousness (*al-ḥirṣ*) and satisfaction (*al-qanāʿa*), miserliness (*al-bukhl*) and openhandedness (*al-jūd*), delight in what is at hand and sorrow over what is lacking, prudent altruism (*al-īthār*) and lavish spending (*al-infāq*), extension and reduction [of wealth], squandering (*al-tabdhīr*) and stinginess (*al-taqtīr*), contentment (*al-riḍā*) with little and disdain (*istiḥqār*) for excess—all of that to test [humankind] regarding which of them is best in deeds, to see which of them prefers [this] world over the hereafter, which of them seeks to turn away from and abandon the hereafter while clinging to [this] world as hoarded treasure and property. 113

May prayers and abundant peace be upon Muḥammad—who with his creed abrogated many a creed and who with his law rendered religions and sects obsolete—and upon his family and Companions, who trod the path of their Lord in humility.

To proceed, the tribulations (*fitan*) of [this] world are many-faceted
114 and manifold, wide of range and of scope. However, wealth and possessions (*al-amwāl*) are the greatest of its tribulations, and the most overwhelming of its ordeals (*miḥan*). Of the tribulations wealth entails, the worst is that no one can do without it, and yet if one has it, there can be no safety from it [and its attendant trials]. That is, if money is lacking, the result is poverty, which can nearly lead to unbelief. And if it is present, the result is tyranny (*al-ṭughyān*), the outcome of which can only be loss.

In sum: Wealth is not without benefits (*al-fawāʾid*) and it is not without harms (*al-āfāt*). Its benefits are among those things that lead to salvation (*al-munjiyyāt*), while its harms are among those things that lead to perdition (*al-mahlikāt*).[1] Distinguishing between [wealth's] evil and its good is a difficult task, achieved only by those with sound insight in the *dīn*, that is, firmly established scholars, not those who are seduced by outward appearance.

Explaining this [matter] in isolation is important. What we mentioned in *The Book on the Censure of the World*[2] was not an examination of wealth specifically, but rather of [this] world (*al-dunya*) in general. [This] world comprises every type of temporal fortune: wealth is one portion of [this] world; fame is a portion; satisfying the desires of the stomach and the genitals is a portion; venting one's wrath onto someone out of anger and envy is another; pride and the quest for prominence are still another. Indeed, [what constitutes this world] has many portions, the common denominator for humankind being temporal fortune.

Our topic of investigation in this book will be wealth alone. Indeed, wealth entails harms and dangers. For humankind, its absence means

1 Eds., *mahlikāt* is the word used in the title of this quarter—*rabīʿ al-mahlikāt*—of the *Iḥyāʾ ʿulūm al-Dīn*, which we have translated as "The Quarter of Perils." Here within the text, the translator draws out the meaning, translating the term as "those things that lead to perdition."

2 Eds., this is the volume of the *Iḥyā* which precedes this one: Book 26 in the entire series and Book 6 in the "Quarter of Perils." See Al-Ghazali, *The Censure of the World*, trans. Abdul Rahman Fitzgerald and Fouad Aresmouk, Louisville, KY: Fons Vitae Publishing, 2023

poverty (*al-faqr*), while its presence means affluence (*al-ghinā*), and these are both conditions through which one is tested and tried.

Thus, for the one who lacks [wealth] there are two [possible] conditions: satisfaction (*al-qanāʿa*) or covetousness (*al-ḥirṣ*), one of which is blameworthy and the other praiseworthy.

For the covetous person (*al-ḥarīṣ*) there are two [possible] con- 115
ditions (*ḥālatān*): greed (*ṭamʿ*) for what others possess, or diligent application to crafts and industries, placing no hope in what others [possess]. Greed is the worse of these two conditions.

Likewise, for person who possesses [wealth] there are two [possible] conditions: withholding (*imsāk*) out of miserliness (*al-bukhl*) and avarice (*al-shuḥḥ*), and willingness to spend (*infāq*). One of these is blameworthy and the other praiseworthy.

For the person who spends [money] there are two [possible] conditions: squandering (*al-tabdhīr*) and moderation (*al-iqtiṣād*). The praiseworthy [condition] is moderation.

These situations are ambiguous (*mutashābiha*). Hence, it is important to clarify the obscurity associated with them. We shall expound on these matters in the course of the following fourteen sections, God سُبْحَانَهُ وَتَعَالَىٰ willing: (1) the censure of wealth (*al-māl*); (2) the praise of [wealth]; (3) detailing the benefits and harms of wealth; (4) the censure of covetousness (*al-ḥirṣ*) and greed (*al-ṭamʿ*); (5) the remedy for covetousness and greed; (6) the virtue of generosity (*al-sakhāʾ*); (7) tales of the generous (*al-askhīyāʾ*); (8) the censure of miserliness (*al-bukhl*); (9) tales of the miserly (*al-bukhalāʾ*); (10) altruism (*al-īthār*) and its virtue; (11) the defining feature of generosity and of miserliness; (12) the remedy for miserliness; (13) the overall functions of wealth; and (14) the censure of affluence and the praise of poverty.

1

An Elucidation of the Censure of Wealth 116
and the Abhorrent Nature of Love for It

God سُبْحَانَهُ وَتَعَالَى says, *O you who have believed, let not your wealth and your children divert you from the remembrance of God. And whoever does that - then those are the losers* [Q. 63:9].

He سُبْحَانَهُ وَتَعَالَى also says, *Your wealth and your children are but a trial (fitna), and Allah has with Him a great reward* [Q. 64:15].

Thus, whoever chooses his wealth and his children over that which he will find with God has cheated himself greatly and has suffered immense loss.

He عَزَّوَجَلَّ also declares, *Whoever desires the life of* [*this*] *world and its adornments - We fully repay them for their deeds therein, and they therein will not be deprived* [Q. 11:15].

He سُبْحَانَهُ وَتَعَالَى says, *No!* [*But*] *indeed, man transgresses, because he sees himself self-sufficient* [Q. 96:6-7].

He سُبْحَانَهُ وَتَعَالَى says, *Competition in* [*worldly*] *increase diverts you* [Q. 102:1].

The Messenger of God صَلَّى ٱللَّهُ عَلَيْهِ وَسَلَّمَ said, "The love of wealth and status (*al-sharaf*) brings forth hypocrisy in the heart, just as water brings forth green plants."[1]

---

1 Al-Ḥāfiẓ al-ʿIrāqī said, "I have not found it with this wording." He then mentioned a version containing the word *jāh* instead of *sharaf* (translated here as "privilege"). *Itḥāf* (8:144).

He صَلَّىٱللَّهُعَلَيْهِوَسَلَّمَ said, "Two ravenous wolves sent into a sheep's enclosure will do it no more harm than the love of status, wealth, and fame will do to the *dīn* of the Muslim."[2]

117 He صَلَّىٱللَّهُعَلَيْهِوَسَلَّمَ said, "Most will perish, except for those of God's servants about whom He said, 'such-and-such and such-and-such,' and their numbers are few."[3]

Someone once asked, "Oh Messenger of God, who [are] the worst of your community [of Muslims] (*umma*)?" He عَلَيْهِٱلصَّلَاةُوَٱلسَّلَامُ said, "The affluent (*al-aghnīyāʾ*)."[4]

He صَلَّىٱللَّهُعَلَيْهِوَسَلَّمَ said, "After you, there will come those who partake of [this] world's finest and most varied pleasures: who ride sleek, powerful horses and the like; who marry the most beautiful women; who wear the softest raiment. They have bellies that a small portion will not satisfy, and souls (*anfus*) which [even] with abundance will not be satisfied. Intent on [this] world, they come and go in its pursuit. They take [this world] as a god apart from their God, as a lord apart from their Lord. They seek it as their be-all and end-all, and to their desires they readily succumb. Thus, it was the firm intention of Muḥammad b. ʿAbdallāh that those of your descendants' descendants, and successors' successors, who live to see that [future] age, should not greet such people, visit their sick, take part in their funeral processions, or venerate their elderly. For those [who do so] have contributed to the destruction of Islam."[5]

---

2 Narrated by al-Tirmidhī (2376) from the *ḥadīth* of Kaʿb b. Mālik رَضِيَٱللَّهُعَنْهُ with the following wording, "Two hungry wolves released among sheep will be no more harmful to them than will a person's covetousness (*ḥirṣ*) for money and privilege will be to his or her spiritual life (*dīn*)." A similar wording is found in al-Ṭabarāni, *al-Awsaṭ* (6275).

3 Narrated by Aḥmad in *al-Musnad* (2:535) from a *ḥadīth* of Abū Hurayra رَضِيَٱللَّهُعَنْهُ. The version that reads, "Those who suffer the greatest loss..." (*al-akhsarūn*), rather than "Most..." (*al-aktharūn*), narrated by al-Bukhārī (6638) and Muslim (990), appeared earlier.

4 This is how it appears in al-Muḥāsibī in *al-Waṣāyā* (70). In *al-Ṣamt wa Ādāb al-Lisān* [Silence and the proprieties of speech] (150), Ibn Abī al-Dunyā gave the following wording from a *ḥadīth* of Fāṭima عَلَيْهَاٱلسَّلَامُ classified as *marfūʿ* (that is, attributed to the Messenger of God and narrated by a Companion): "The most evil of my community [of Muslims] are those who have grown up in the lap of luxury, who eat all varieties of food and wear all varieties of clothing, and who speak in a boastful, affected manner."

5 This is how it appears in al-Muḥāsibī in *al-Waṣāyā* (96) in its full version. Part of it was included by al-Ṭabarānī in *al-Kabīr* (8:107) and by Abū Nuʿaym in *al-Ḥilya*

[The Prophet] صَلَّى ٱللَّهُ عَلَيْهِ وَسَلَّمَ also said, "Leave [this] world to the 118
people of it. Whoever takes more than he needs from [this] world brings about his own destruction, though he realizes it not."[6]

He صَلَّى ٱللَّهُ عَلَيْهِ وَسَلَّمَ also said, "The son of Adam says, 'My wealth, my wealth!' [So tell me, O son of Adam]: What do you possess of your wealth other than what you have consumed, and which therefore is gone? Or what you have dressed yourselves in which is now worn out? Or [is it, in fact, only] that which you have freely given away as charity which is lasting?"[7]

A man once said, "O Messenger of God, why is it that I do not love death?" He صَلَّى ٱللَّهُ عَلَيْهِ وَسَلَّمَ said, "Do you have wealth?" [The man] replied, "Yes, O Messenger of God." He صَلَّى ٱللَّهُ عَلَيْهِ وَسَلَّمَ said to him, "Offer up your wealth [to God], for the believer's heart is with his wealth. If he offers it up [to God], he will want to join it, and if he leaves it behind, he will want to remain behind with it."[8]

He صَلَّى ٱللَّهُ عَلَيْهِ وَسَلَّمَ also said, "The son of Adam has three dear friends. One of them follows him until his spirit is gathered in [death]; the second follows him to his grave; and the third follows him to his resurrection. The one which follows him until his spirit is gathered in [death] is his wealth. The one which follows him to his grave is his family. And the one which follows him to his resurrection is his actions."[9]

(*Ḥilyat al-Awliyāʾ wa Ṭabaqāt al-Aṣfiyāʾ*) [The beauty of the righteous and the ranks of the elite] (6:90) taken from the *ḥadīth* of Abū Umāma. The *ḥadīth* concerned reads as follows: "People belonging to my community [of Muslims] will eat all manner of foods, imbibe all manner of drinks, wear all manner of raiment, and speak in an arrogant, affected manner. These are of the evil ones of my community [of Muslims]."

6 Narrated by al-Bazzār in his *Musnad* (6444) from a *ḥadīth* of Anas رَضِيَ ٱللَّهُ عَنْهُ. This version of the *ḥadīth* contains the phrase *jīfa* (corpse) in lieu of *ḥatf* (destruction). The same wording as that found here is used by Tammām in his *Fawāʾid* (1621) and by Ibn ʿAsākir in *Tārīkh Dimashq* [The history of Damascus] (55:191).

7 Narrated by Muslim (2958).

8 Narrated by Ibn al-Mubārak in *al-Zuhd* (634).

9 Narrated by al-Bazzār in his *Musnad* (8356) and by al-Bayhaqī in *al-Shuʿab* (9993) from a *ḥadīth* of Abu Hurayra رَضِيَ ٱللَّهُ عَنْهُ. It was also included by al-Bukhārī (6514) and Muslim (2960) from the *ḥadīth* of Anas رَضِيَ ٱللَّهُ عَنْهُ which reads, "There are three that follow the dead. Two turn back, and one remains with them. They are followed by their family, their wealth, and their actions. Their family and wealth turn back, while their actions remain."

119 The disciples of Jesus عَلَيْهِ ٱلسَّلَامُ once asked him, "Why is it that you are able to walk on water, while we are not?" He said to them, "What value do you place on the dinar and the dirham?" They said, "A high value." He said, "To me they are no more than a clod of dirt, an evil thing."[10]

Salmān al-Fārisī wrote to Abū l-Dardāʾ,[11] saying, "My brother, beware, lest you amass in [this] world that for which you do not give thanks. For I heard the Messenger of God صَلَّىٱللَّهُعَلَيْهِوَسَلَّمَ say, 'The person who possessed worldly goods and who obeyed God with respect to these possessions will be brought [on the day of resurrection] with his wealth between his hands. Whenever the *ṣirāṭ*[12] sways beneath him, his wealth will say to him, "Go forth, for you have fulfilled your duty towards God with respect to me." Then the person who possessed worldly goods, but who did not obey God with respect to [these possessions], will be brought with his wealth between his shoulders. Whenever the *ṣirāṭ* sways beneath him, his wealth will say to him, "Woe to you! Why did you not fulfill your duty to God with respect to me?" And it will continue to do so until [that person], in distress, bursts into loud laments.'"[13]

Everything that we cited in *The Book On Poverty and Abstinence* in the way of censuring affluence and praising poverty all relates back to the censure of wealth.[14] Consequently, we will not repeat at length what was stated there. The same is true of what we cited in
120 *The Book on The Censure of the World*, since this was also a censuring of wealth by way of inclusion; for wealth is the principal pillar of

10 Narrated by Ibn Abī al-Dunyā in *al-Yaqīn* (40) on the authority of al-Fuḍayl b. ʿIyāḍ.

11 This is how the text reads in the various manuscripts, whereas in fact, the letter was written by Abū l-Dardāʾ to Salmān رَضِيَٱللَّهُعَنْهُمَا, as can be seen in the sources from which the report was taken. This was also affirmed by al-Ḥāfiẓ al-ʿIrāqī. See *al-Itḥāf* (8:146).

12 Trans.: The bridge, fine as a razor's edge, over which all who enter the garden must pass.

13 Narrated by ʿAbd al-Razzāq in *al-Muṣannaf* [A compilation of *ḥadīth*s about the righteous predecessors according to subject and without regard for authenticity] (11:96), by Ibn Abī al-Dunyā in *al-Zuhd* (340), by Abū Nuʿaym in *al-Ḥilya* (1:214), and by al-Bayhaqī in *al-Shuʿab* (10174).

14 Eds.: This is book 34 of the *Iḥyā* and is published in English translation: al-Ghazali, *On Poverty and Abstinence: Book 34 of the Revival of the Religious Sciences*, trans. Anthony F. Shaker, Cambridge, UK: Islamic Texts Society, 2019

[this] world. Rather, we will speak now of that which has to do with wealth specifically.

[The Messenger of God] صَلَّى ٱللَّهُ عَلَيْهِ وَسَلَّمَ said, "When a servant of God dies, the angels ask, 'What did he send ahead of him [to God]?,' while people ask, 'What did he leave behind?'"[15]

He صَلَّى ٱللَّهُ عَلَيْهِ وَسَلَّمَ also said, "Do not choose loss by loving [this] world."[16]

***

Traditions (*āthār*)

It has been said that a man once harmed and demonstrated evil toward Abū l-Dardāʾ, who [in turn] said, "Oh God, whoever does me harm, give him good physical health, a long life, and abundant wealth."[17] Note how Abū l-Dardāʾ viewed abundant wealth as the worst possible affliction—along with physical health and long life—since they are bound to lead to tyranny.

ʿAlī رَضِيَ ٱللَّهُ عَنْهُ once placed a dirham in his palm and said, "Unless you leave my possession, you will do me no good."[18]

> It has been said that when ʿUmar رَضِيَ ٱللَّهُ عَنْهُ sent Zaynab bt. 121
> Jaḥsh her share,[19] she said, "What is this?"
>
> She was told, "It was sent to you by ʿUmar b. al-Khaṭṭāb."
>
> And she said, "May God forgive him." Then she took down a curtain of hers, cut it up into pieces and made them into money bags, and then divided [her share] among the members of her household, her blood relations, and their orphans. Afterwards she raised her hands, and said, "Oh God, let not ʿUmar's gift reach me after this year." She was the

15 Narrated by Ibn Abī Shayba in *al-Muṣannaf* (35851) and by al-Bayhaqī in *al-Shuʿab* (9992) on the authority of Abū Hurayra رَضِيَ ٱللَّهُ عَنْهُ.

16 Narrated by al-Tirmidhī (2328) with the use of the phrase *fa targhabū* (by desiring) instead of *fa tuḥibbū* (by loving).

17 This prayer of his was narrated by Abū Nuʿaym in *al-Ḥilya* (2:91) on the authority of ʿĀmir b. ʿAbdallāh b. ʿAbd Qays. Al-Ḥāfiẓ al-Zabīdī said in his *Itḥāf* (8:147), "It was transmitted by the author of *al-Qūt*."

18 Transmitted by the author of *al-Qūt*. *Al-Itḥāf* (8:147).

19 Trans.: that is, her share of the treasures won in the Muslims' wars with the Persians.

> first of the Messenger of God's صَلَّى ٱللَّهُ عَلَيْهِ وَسَلَّمَ wives to follow him [in death].[20]

Al-Ḥasan said, "By God, no one has exalted the dirham but that they have been abased by God سُبْحَانَهُ وَتَعَالَىٰ."[21]

It has been said that when the dinar and the dirham were first struck, Iblīs raised them up, pressed them to his forehead, then kissed them and said, "Whoever loves you will truly be my slave."[22]

Shumayṭ b. ʿAjlān said, "The dinar and the dirham are the nose-ropes by which the hypocrites are led away to the fire."[23]

Yaḥyā b. Muʿādh said, "The dirham is a scorpion. If you fail to protect yourself against it with the proper *ruqya*,[24] do not take it into your possession. For if it stings you, its venom will kill you." He was then asked, "And what is the *ruqya* that will protect against it?" He replied, "To take it from lawful sources, and to place it where it rightfully belongs."[25]

122 Al-ʿAlāʾ b. Ziyād said, "[This] world appeared to me in all its finest adornment. And I said, 'I seek refuge in God from your evil.' It replied, 'If you wish that God grant you refuge from my evil, then come to hate the dirham.'"[26]

This is because the dinar and the dirham make up the entirety of [this] worldly life, since it is through them that we gain access to all spheres of [this] world. Thus, those who steadfastly resist them can steadfastly resist [this] world. On this point someone once said,[27]

> I have found that the true measure of devoutness (*al-tawarruʿ*)
> Is how one relates to money.
>
> For if you obtain it, then let it go,
> And know that you possess the piety (*al-taqwā*) of a Muslim.

---

20 Narrated by Ibn Saʿd in his *Ṭabaqāt* (10:106).

21 Narrated by al-Bayhaqī in *al-Zuhd al-Kabīr* (281).

22 Narrated by Abū Nuʿaym in *al-Ḥilya* (1:328) on the authority of Ibn ʿAbbās رَضِيَ ٱللَّهُ عَنْهُمَا.

23 Narrated by Abū Nuʿaym in *al-Ḥilya* (3:128).

24 Eds.: Recitation of specific *āyāt* of the Qurʾān, or prayers from *ḥadīth*, generally for protection and healing.

25 Narrated by Abū Nuʿaym in *al-Ḥilya* (10:60) without the question.

26 Narrated by Ibn Abī Shayba in *al-Muṣannaf* (31158).

27 These lines of poetry are attributed to Sufyān al-Thawrī. See *Muʿjam al-Udabāʾ* [Dictionary of litterateurs] (1:100).

On this matter it has also been said:[28]

> Be not deceived
> by a person's patched garment,
>
> A robe whose hem rises
> far above the ankle,
>
> Or a forehead bearing
> the marks of prostration.
>
> Rather, observe whether the dirham's owner
> is dazzled by it, or cautious.

It is said:

Maslama b. ʿAbd al-Malik went in to see ʿUmar b. ʿAbd
al-ʿAzīz رَحِمَهُ ٱللَّهُ when he was dying. And [Maslama] said, "Oh
Commander of the Faithful, you have done a deed that no 123
one before you has ever done. You have left your children
with neither dinar nor dirham." And he [the caliph] had
thirteen sons.

ʿUmar replied, "Help me sit upright." So, they sat him upright. Then he said, "As for your claim that I have left them neither dinar nor dirham, I have never deprived them of any of their rights, nor have I granted them a right that was due another. Rather, each of my sons will be of one of two types. Either he will be a man who obeys God, in which case God will be his sufficiency, for God watches over the righteous. Or he will be a man who disobeys God, in which case I care not what happens [to him]."[29]

It has been related that Muḥammad b. Kaʿb al Quraẓī amassed great wealth.

Someone then said to him, "[It would be best] if you saved it up for your children after you."

28 These verses are found in *al-Mudhish* [The amazing] (1:211) without attribution.

29 Narrated by Abū Nuʿaym in *al-Ḥilya* (5:333) with a similar wording.

He replied, "No. Rather, I am saving it up for myself with my Lord [by giving it away in charity], and [bequeathing] the fortune that is my Lord to my children."[30]

It is related that a man once said to Abū ʿAbd Rabb, "O brother, do not depart [from this world] in evil, while leaving that which is good behind for your children." So Abū ʿAbd Rabb donated one hundred thousand dirhams [in charity].[31]

Yaḥyā b. Muʿādh said,

"There are two disasters the likes of which neither the ancients nor the last to live will have heard of, and which [pertain to] a person's wealth at the time of his death."

It was asked, "And what are they?"

He replied, "For all of it to be taken from him, and for him to be held accountable for it all."[32]

***

30 Narrated by al-Bayhaqī in *al-Zuhd al-Kabīr* (436).

31 Narrated by Abū Nuʿaym in *al-Ḥilya* (5:160) with a similar wording. Abū ʿAbd Rabb was ʿUbayda b. Muhājir.

32 Narrated by al-Khaṭīb in *al-Zuhd* (11).

2

An Elucidation of the Praise of Wealth, and of its Praise Combined with its Censure 124

KNOW that God سُبْحَانَهُ وَتَعَالَىٰ calls wealth good in some passages of the Qurʾān. He عَزَّ وَجَلَّ says, *Prescribed for you when death approaches* [*any*] *one of you if he leaves wealth* [*is that he should make*] *a bequest for the parents and near relatives according to what is acceptable – a duty upon the righteous* [Q. 2:180].

The Messenger of God صَلَّى ٱللَّٰهُ عَلَيْهِ وَسَلَّمَ said, "Righteous wealth blesses the righteous man."[1]

Everything said about the reward for charity (*ṣadaqa*) and the *ḥajj* is, in essence, in commendation of wealth, since neither of these [acts of worship] could be performed without it.

As [God] سُبْحَانَهُ وَتَعَالَىٰ says, [*And as for the wall, it belonged to two orphan boys in the city, and there was beneath it a treasure for them, and their father had been righteous. So your Lord intended that they reach maturity*] *and extract their treasure, as a mercy from your Lord* [Q. 18:82].

Enumerating the gifts He grants to His servants, God سُبْحَانَهُ وَتَعَالَىٰ said, [*He will send* [*rain from*] *the sky upon you in* [*continuing*] *showers,*] *and give you increase in wealth and children and provide for you gardens and provide for you rivers* [Q. 71:11-12].

1 Narrated by Aḥmad in *al-Musnad* (4:197), and by Ibn Ḥibbān in his *Ṣaḥīḥ* (3210).

He صَلَّى ٱللَّهُ عَلَيْهِ وَسَلَّمَ said, "Poverty can nearly lead to unbelief,"[2] a statement which entails a commendation of wealth.

You cannot comprehend the combination of the praise and censure [of wealth] except by realizing the wisdom of wealth, its purpose, its harms, and its dangers. In this way you will be able to
125 see that it is good in one respect and evil in another respect, and that insofar as it [wealth] is good, it is praiseworthy, and insofar as it is evil, it is blameworthy. Hence, it is neither purely good nor purely evil. Rather, it is a cause of both [good and evil]. Anything of which this can be said will inevitably deserve to be praised at times, and censured at others, but those blessed with insight and discernment know how to distinguish its praiseworthy aspects from its blameworthy ones.

[This topic] will be elucidated by drawing upon what we mentioned in *The Book on Thankfulness* in [the section on] the elucidation of the boons (*al-khayrāt*), as well as in the [section] detailing the various degrees of blessings.[3]

The sufficient gist of [what was discussed there] is that the goal of the sagacious and those possessed of insight is the happiness of the hereafter, which is abiding bliss and everlasting tenure; and it is towards this goal that the honorable and the sagacious persevere. The Messenger of God صَلَّى ٱللَّهُ عَلَيْهِ وَسَلَّمَ was once asked, "Who is the noblest and wisest of all people?" And he said, "Those who most frequently remember death, and those who are best prepared for it."[4]

This happiness can only be achieved in [this] world by three means, which are:

- Virtues of the soul, such as knowledge and good manners
- Virtues of the body, such as health and wellbeing
- Virtues that are external to the body, such as wealth and all other causes [of wealth and external support]

---

2 Narrated by Abū al-Shaykh in *al-Tawbīkh wa-l-Tanbīh* [Reprimand and warning] (74), by Abū al-Nuʿaym in *al-Ḥilya* (3:53), and by al-Bayhaqī in *al-Shuʿab* (6188) from a *ḥadīth* of Anas رَضِيَ ٱللَّهُ عَنْهُ.

3 Eds.: This is Book 32 of the *Iḥyā* and has been translated into English: al-Ghazali, *On Patience and Thankfulness: Book 32 of the Revival of the Religious Sciences*, trans. H.T. Littlejohn, Cambridge, UK: Islamic Texts Society, 2010.

4 Narrated by Ibn Mājah (4259).

The highest of these are [the virtues] of the soul, followed by those
of the body, while those that are external to the body are the basest
of them. Wealth is classed among the external virtues, the lowest
of which are the dirham and the dinar [i.e., money itself], both
of which are servants, and themselves have no servants. They are
desired for the sake of other things, not for their own sake. Thus,
the soul (*nafs*) is the intrinsic nature (*al-jawhar*) whose happiness 126
is sought. For [the soul] attends to knowledge, understanding, and
virtuous morals in order to attain them as innate traits in its essence.
And the body serves the soul by means of its senses and organs,
while food and clothing [in turn] serve the body. It has been stated
previously that the purpose of food is to ensure the survival of the
body, that of marriage is to preserve progeny, and that of the body is
the completion of the soul (*takmīl al-nafs*), as well as its purification
and adornment by way of knowledge and good character.

Whoever understands this order will realize the value of wealth and its noble aspect. For insofar as [money] is a necessity in order to secure food and clothing—which, in turn, are necessities for the survival of the body, which itself is a necessity for the perfection of the soul—it is good. And whoever knows a thing's benefit, its end, and its purpose, and uses it for the sake of that end, ever bearing it in mind and never losing sight of it, does well and attains benefit. For that which achieves a good aim is itself praiseworthy.

Hence, wealth is a tool and a means to a valid end. However, it may also be used as a tool and a means to achieving corrupt ends, by which we mean those ends which hinder [achievement of] the bliss of the hereafter, blocking the path of knowledge and [beneficial] action. [Wealth] is, therefore, both praiseworthy and blameworthy. It is praiseworthy when associated with a praiseworthy purpose, and blameworthy when associated with a blameworthy purpose. "For whoever takes from [this] world more than he needs contributes to his own destruction, though he realizes it not," as stated in the report [cited earlier]."[5]

Given that human beings' natural propensity is to succumb to 127
desires that block the path to God, and that wealth facilitates [this

5 Narrated by al-Bazzār in his *Musnad* (6444) from a *ḥadīth* of Anas رَضِيَ اللَّهُ عَنْهُ, by Tammām in his *Fawāʾid* (1621), and by Ibn ʿAsākir in *Tārīkh Dimashq* (55:191).

propensity] and is a tool in its service, there is all the more danger in possessing more of it than the amount that is sufficient. Consequently, the prophets عَلَيْهِمُ ٱلسَّلَامُ prayed for protection from its evil. Indeed, our Prophet صَلَّى ٱللَّهُ عَلَيْهِ وَسَلَّمَ said, "Oh God, cause the sustenance (*qūt*) of Muḥammad's household to be sufficient and no more (*kafāf*)."[6]

He only asked of [this] world that which would yield good.

He صَلَّى ٱللَّهُ عَلَيْهِ وَسَلَّمَ said, "Oh God, cause me to live poor and die poor (*miskīn*), and raise me up [on the day of resurrection] in the company of the poor (*al-masākīn*)."[7]

Abraham صَلَّى ٱللَّهُ عَلَيْهِ وَسَلَّمَ sought refuge, saying, *My Lord, make this city* [*i.e., Mecca*] *secure and keep me and my sons away from worshipping idols* [Q. 14:35]. By ["idols"], he meant the substances of gold and silver. After all, a prophet would never be in danger of believing that divinity could inhere in any [material] thing [made] from these substances. Indeed, even before they receive their call to prophethood—from childhood—prophets are prevented from worshipping them.

And the meaning of "worshipping them" is loving them, being dazzled by them, and putting one's trust in them.

Our Prophet صَلَّى ٱللَّهُ عَلَيْهِ وَسَلَّمَ said, "The slave of the dinar will suffer misery, and the slave of the dirham will suffer misery. He will suffer misery and will not recover. And if he is pricked [with the
128 thorn that is the love of money], it will not be pulled out."[8] The Prophet عَلَيْهِ ٱلصَّلَاةُ وَٱلسَّلَامُ thus elucidated that whoever loves them [i.e., the dirham and the dinar], is a slave to them. Someone who is a slave of a substance is an idol worshipper. Indeed, whoever is a slave to anything or anyone other than God is an idol worshipper. That is, whoever is thereby cut off from God سُبْحَانَهُ وَتَعَالَىٰ and [the performance of] his duties toward God is like an idol worshipper,

6 Narrated by al-Bukhārī (6460) and Muslim (1055), whose versions contain the word *qūt* instead of *kafāf*. It was narrated with the same wording as that found here by Ibn Ḥibbān in his *Ṣaḥīḥ* (6343).

7 Narrated by al-Tirmidhī (2352) and Ibn Mājah (4126).

8 Narrated by al-Bukhārī (2887) and Ibn Mājah (4136), whose versions read "will suffer misery and setback" (*taʿisa wa-intakas*) instead of "will suffer misery and never recover" (*taʿisa wa lā intaʿasha*). In his work entitled, *Taṣḥīfāt al-muḥaddithīn* [Misplacements of diacritical marks by *ḥadīth* transmitters] (1:299), al-ʿAskarī lists *intaʿasha* (to recover, rise from a fall) as a misspelling or corruption of *intaqasha* (to extract, as a thorn).

and this is *shirk* [i.e., the association of partners with God]. However, *shirk* takes two forms: covert *shirk,* which does not merit eternity in the fire, and of which believers are rarely able to free themselves entirely—and this is more subtle than the creeping of an ant. And overt *shirk,* which does merit eternity in the fire. We seek refuge with God from all of it.

***

3

129 ## An Elucidation Detailing the Harms of Wealth and its Benefits

KNOW that wealth is like a viper that produces both venom and an antidote. Its benefits are the antidote, while its calamities are the venom.

Whosoever knows its calamities and its benefits will be able to guard against its evil while allowing its goodness to flow forth.

***

The benefits [of wealth] fall into two categories: worldly and spiritual.

As for the worldly [benefits], there is no need to mention them, since they are known to all. Otherwise, you would not find people devoting themselves so eagerly to obtaining it.

As for its spiritual benefits, they can all be divided into three types.

The first type [of spiritual benefit to be had from wealth] consists of [benefits which arise from] spending it on oneself: for example, one might spend it on acts of worship, or to assist acts of worship. As for acts of worship, this is, for example, assisting [acts such as] the *ḥajj* or *jihād*. For one cannot engage in these except by means of wealth. And these are among the most important means of drawing closer to God, while the poor person is prohibited from [attaining] the merit they bring.

Someone might also [spend his wealth on] that which provides the strength required for worship, including food, clothing, shelter, marriage, and the basic necessities of life. For if these necessities are not readily available, the heart's attention will be diverted to efforts to secure them. And thus, he will not be free to devote himself to the *dīn*. Whatever is required in order to enable worship, is itself a form of worship. 130

Thus, obtaining what [a person] needs from [this] world in order to carry out his *dīn* is one of the spiritual benefits [of wealth]. However, this does not include luxuries and overabundance. For these are classed solely among worldly fortunes.

***

The second type [of spiritual benefit to be had from wealth] consists of [benefits that arise from] spending it on others.

And this falls under four categories: charity (*ṣadaqa*), chivalry [and social graces] (*al-murūwʾa*), the preservation of reputation, and wages paid for services rendered.

As for charity, its reward is not obscure. Furthermore, it quenches the wrath of the Lord عَزَّوَجَلَّ. We mentioned its virtues earlier.

As for chivalry [and social graces], by this we mean: the practice of spending money on the affluent and well-placed in society via hospitality, gifts, assistance, and the like. This form of spending could not be referred to as charity, for charity refers only to what one gives over the needy. Nevertheless, this [form of giving] is also among the spiritual benefits, since by means of it the servant [of God] gains friends and spiritual brethren, and achieves the quality of generosity (*al-sakhāʾ*) and joins the company of the generous. For only those who extend good deeds and walk the path of honorable behavior and chivalry can be described as openhanded. This type of comportment also brings a great reward, since we possess numerous reports which speak of gifts, acts of hospitality, and feeding others without the recipients' necessarily being poor or needy.

As for the preservation of reputation, by this we mean giving freely of [one's] wealth to ward off satire by poets and slander by insolent fools, thereby silencing them and repelling their evil. This [protection] constitutes an immediate benefit from among the temporal of the spiritual fortunes. The Messenger of God صَلَّىٱللَّهُعَلَيْهِوَسَلَّمَ said, "That which a person spends in defense of his reputation shall 131 be counted in his favor as charity (*ṣadaqa*)."[1] And how could it be otherwise, when it helps to prevent backbiters from committing the act of disobedience that is backbiting, and guards against the speech of enmity that is stirred up, which in turn leads to acts of ego-gratification and revenge that themselves transgress the limits of the law?!

As for [the benefits of spending one's money on wages for] services, this is [based on the fact] that the tasks that the human being needs to perform in order to manage his affairs are many. And if he performed them himself, there would be no time left, making it difficult to walk the path of the hereafter through contemplation and divine remembrance, which constitute the most sublime stations of the spiritual seeker. Whoever has no wealth is thus obliged to serve himself by buying food, preparing it, cleaning his house, and even copying by hand the books he needs. Someone else could do all of that for you, thereby achieving these goals in your stead. You wrong yourself if you do these things unassisted. By contrast, learning, [beneficial] action, contemplation, and divine remembrance [are things that] no one else can conceivably do on your behalf. So, wasting your time on anything but these [pursuits] would be an immense loss.

***

The third type [of spiritual benefit to be had from wealth arises from] what one spends, not on a particular person, but rather for a general good:

Such as the construction of mosques, bridges, inns for travellers,
132 hospices, and water reservoirs along roadways, and other such endowments devoted to the public welfare. [Such endowments,] moreover, are lasting goods, as they continue to yield good after one's death, not to mention the blessing of the [resultant] supplications of the righteous for a long time to come. By these you attain a high degree of good.

These are the various benefits of wealth in the *dīn* which are tied to temporal fortunes: deliverance from the humiliation of begging

1 Narrated by al-Dāraquṭnī in his *Sunan* (3:28), and by al-Ḥākim in *al-Mustadrak ʿalā al-Ṣaḥīḥayn* [A five-volume *ḥadīth* collection which its author said contained only *ḥadīths* which were authentic by the standards of Muslim, al-Bukhārī, or both] (2:50).

and the degradation of poverty; [gaining] others' respect and admiration; [gaining] an abundance of friends, helpers, spiritual brethren; and [gaining] dignity and nobility in the hearts. All of these are among the worldly fortunes that wealth brings.

***

Turning now to the harms [that wealth can cause]: some are worldly, while others are spiritual.

As for the spiritual [harms], there are three.

The first: it lures [people] into acts of disobedience:

The desires (*shahawāt*) are interdependent and mutually reinforcing. Now, weakness may determine between being upright and committing an act of disobedience, by preventing the committing [of the act of disobedience]. But despite the human being unable to commit the act of disobedience, the motivation to do so will remain. However, if the ability to commit it is felt, the motivation to do so will be quickened. And wealth is an enabling factor which agitates the motivation for the acts of disobedience and can provide the occasion for their being committed. If someone rushes headlong
into what he craves, he will perish. If, on the other hand, someone 133
forbears patiently, he will suffer hardship. Hence, patience combined with the ability to commit an act of disobedience is more trying [than not having the ability to do so in the first place]. Thus, the tribulation (*fitna*) of prosperity is more severe than the tribulation of disadvantage.

The second: [wealth] lures [people] into luxuries that are neutral (*mubāḥāt*)[2]:

This is the lowest of degrees. For what person with wealth will be able to go on eating barley bread, wearing coarse garments, and abstaining from delicacies the way Sulaymān b. Dāwūd عَلَيْهِمَا السَّلَامُ was able to do during his reign? Rather, the best of states [for the wealthy person] is to indulge in what [this] world has to offer. He thus accustoms himself to this [way of life] to the point where luxuries become habitual, beloved by him, he finds himself unable to do without them, and one pleasure leads to another.

2 Eds.: That is, acts that are permissible but for which neither reward nor punishment is to be expected.

If someone's fondness for [worldly comforts] grows too intense, he may find himself unable to be satisfied with what he can obtain via lawful (*ḥalāl*) means, in which case he may embark on questionable activities (*shubhāt*), put on airs, and engage in flattery, lying, hypocrisy, and all manner of immoral behavior, so as to maintain his worldly status and go on enjoying his luxuries. Whoever has an abundance of wealth comes to have a greater need for people, and whoever needs people is bound to be hypocritical towards them, and to disobey God سُبْحَانَهُ وَتَعَالَىٰ in pursuit of others' approval. Even if someone is spared the first harm—that is, to say, engaging in prohibited activities—he will not be spared these others. For out of the need for other human beings grows both enmity and friendship, which then paves the way for envy, resentment, ostentation, arrogance, lying, backbiting, gossip, and all other acts of disobedience that pertain to the heart and the tongue. Furthermore, [these acts of disobedience] are prone to go beyond [the heart and the tongue] to other members of the body. All of this is an inevitable outcome of the curse of wealth, and of the need to hold on to it and maintain it.

134 The third: this is something from which no one is spared, namely, that taking care of our wealth will distract us from the remembrance of God سُبْحَانَهُ وَتَعَالَىٰ:

All that distracts the servant from God is an immense loss. Therefore, Jesus عَلَيْهِ ٱلسَّلَامُ said, "Wealth entails three harms: the first is that one may obtain it in an unlawful manner." Someone then asked, "And if one obtains it in a lawful manner?" And he said, "[It is that] one will put to an unlawful use." Someone then asked, "And if one puts it to a lawful use?" And he said, "[It is] that looking after it will distract him from God سُبْحَانَهُ وَتَعَالَىٰ."[3]

This is an incurable malady. For the foundation of all forms of worship, their essence, and their secret is the remembrance of God سُبْحَانَهُ وَتَعَالَىٰ and the contemplation of His majesty, which requires an unburdened and present heart. The owner of a landed estate will be thinking day and night about how to bring suit against the peasantry and settle accounts with them; how to seek redress against partners and raise disputes with them over water and borders; how to contest

3 Narrated by al-Bayhaqī in *al-Zuhd al-Kabīr* (248) on the authority of Sufyān Ibn Saʿīd.

with government officials over the land tax; how to file complaints against laborers over their faulty construction work; and how to take action against farmers for their betrayal and theft. Similarly, the merchant will be preoccupied with whether his partner has betrayed him and taken all the profit for himself, his failure to conduct his business properly, and his waste of money. And the same goes for the owner of livestock and all other types of wealth. It is thus with all kinds of wealth. Of these, the type that requires the least effort [and preoccupation] would be money buried underground. Yet even then, one's thoughts will continue to revolve around it: how to protect it, the fear that someone will find it, and how to keep it out of the hands of those with ambitious desires. There is no end to the paths our minds can go down when we fret over our worldly affairs. However, those who have just enough for each day are safe from all of this.

This is a summary of the earthly harms endured by those who 135
own wealth in [this] world: fear, grief, distress, worry, the hardship of warding off the envious, and the suffering from the hardship of retaining wealth and acquiring it.

Hence, the antidote to wealth is to take what we need for our daily sustenance and spend what remains on doing good. Anything in excess of this will entail venom[4] and harm. We ask God سُبْحَانَهُ وَتَعَالَىٰ for safety, and to assist us out of His bounteous grace. For over this He is abundantly capable.

***

4 Eds.: Referring back to the beginning of this chapter in which the author writes that "wealth is like a viper that produces both venom and an antidote."

4

136 An Elucidation of the Censure of Covetousness (*al-ḥirṣ*) and Greed (*al-ṭamʿ*), and [Elucidation] of the Praise for Satisfaction (*al-qanāʿa*) and Placing No Hope in What Others Possess

Know this: poverty is praiseworthy, as we stated in *The Book on Poverty* [*and Abstinence*]. However, the poor person must be satisfied, disconnected from any greed (*al-ṭamʿ*) for created things giving no regard to what is in others' possession. Nor should he be covetous of acquiring wealth of any kind. However, he can only achieve this by being content with the amount he needs by way of food, clothing, and shelter, limiting himself to the bare minimum, and to the humblest quality thereof. Furthermore, he must limit his hopes to this day or this month, and not preoccupy his heart with anything beyond a month.

If someone looks out longingly for surplus or holds out hopes for the distant future, he forfeits the glory of satisfaction, and is inevitably sullied by greed and the degradation of covetousness. He is drawn by covetousness and greed into vile morals and into the committing of shameful acts that violate virtuous behavior. To human beings, covetousness, greed, and lack of satisfaction come all too naturally.

The Messenger of God صَلَّى ٱللَّهُ عَلَيْهِ وَسَلَّمَ said, "If a son of Adam had two valleys of gold, he would want a third. The son of Adam will never be satisfied as long as he lives. But God accepts the repentance of all who repent."[1]

> Abū Wāqid al-Laythī said,
>
> When the Messenger of God صَلَّى ٱللَّهُ عَلَيْهِ وَسَلَّمَ received revelation, we would come to him for him to teach us what had been revealed to him.
>
> One day I came to him, and he said, "God عَزَّوَجَلَّ says, 137
> 'We have sent down wealth for the performance of ritual prayer and the distribution of charity. And if a son of Adam has one valley of gold, he will wish he had two, and if he has two valleys [filled with the same], he will wish he had a third. The son of Adam will never be satisfied as long as he lives. But God accepts the repentance of all who repent.'"[2]

Abū Mūsā al-Ashʿarī said, "A *sūra* like *Barāʾah*[3] was revealed, after which it was withdrawn. Out of it, however, the following was preserved: 'God upholds this religion through disgraceful peoples. If a son of Adam has two valleys filled with riches, he will wish he had a third. The son of Adam will never be satisfied as long as he lives. But God accepts the repentance of all who repent.'"[4]

He صَلَّى ٱللَّهُ عَلَيْهِ وَسَلَّمَ said, "Two types of insatiable human beings: those who crave knowledge, and those who crave wealth."[5]

He صَلَّى ٱللَّهُ عَلَيْهِ وَسَلَّمَ said, "The son of Adam grows old, but out of him spring two things that are ever young: hope [for things of this world], and the love of money."[6] Given the fact that this is a human disposition that leads people astray, a destructive peril, God
سُبْحَانَهُ وَتَعَالَىٰ and His Messenger صَلَّى ٱللَّهُ عَلَيْهِ وَسَلَّمَ have praised satisfaction 138

1 Narrated by al-Bukhārī (6436, 6439) and Muslim (1048, 1049).

2 Narrated by Abū ʿUbayd in *Faḍāʾil al-Qurʾān* (322), by Aḥmad in *al-Musnad* (5:218), by al-Ṭabarānī in *al-Kabīr* (3:247), and by al-Bayhaqī in *al-Shuʿab* (9800).

3 Trans.: That is, *Sūra* 9, *al-Tawbah*.

4 Narrated by Abū ʿUbayd in *Faḍāʾil al-Qurʾān* (323) with the wording above. The original wording is found in Muslim (1050).

5 Narrated by al-Ḥākim in *al-Mustadrak* (1:92) from a *ḥadīth* of Anas with the following wording, "Two types [of human beings] will never be satisfied. Those who crave knowledge will never be satisfied, and those who craving [this] world will never be satisfied."

6 Narrated by al-Bukhārī (6421) and Muslim (1047).

(*al-qanāʿa*). He ﷺ said, "Blessed is he who is led to Islam and who, having exactly what he needs, is satisfied with this."[7]

And he ﷺ said, "There is no one, rich or poor, who does not wish on the day of resurrection that he had been given mere sufficiency in [this] world."[8]

He ﷺ also said, "True riches do not consist in an abundance of non-essential things; rather, true riches are the riches of the soul."[9]

He ﷺ prohibited excessive covetousness and acquisitiveness. He ﷺ said, "Listen, O people, be moderate in what you seek to acquire, for no one can obtain more than what has been written for him, nor will anyone depart from [this] world without having received what was written for him therein, even if it was strongly resisted."[10]

> It is said:
>
> Moses عَلَيْهِ ٱلسَّلَامُ asked his Lord سُبْحَانَهُ وَتَعَالَىٰ, "Which of your servants is the richest?"
>
> And He said, "The one who is most satisfied with what I have given him."
>
> Then Moses asked, "Which of them is the most just?"
>
> And God replied, "The one who is fair even at his own expense."[11]

139 Ibn Masʿūd رَضِيَ ٱللَّهُ عَنْهُ said, "The Messenger of God ﷺ said, 'The Holy Spirit breathed into me the understanding that no soul shall die without having received its sustenance in full. So fear God and be moderate in what you seek.'"[12]

---

7 Narrated by al-Tirmidhī (2349), by al-Nasāʾī in *al-Sunan al-Kubrā* (9793) from a *ḥadīth* of Fuḍāla b. ʿUbayd رَضِيَ ٱللَّهُ عَنْهُ, and by Muslim (1054) from a *ḥadīth* of ʿAbdallāh b. ʿAmr with the wording: "Happy are those who surrender to God in Islam, upon whom God has bestowed sufficiency, and whom God has caused to be content with what He has given them."

8 Narrated by Ibn Mājah (4140).

9 Narrated by al-Bukhārī (6446) and Muslim (1051).

10 Al-Ḥākim narrated a similar account in *al-Mustadrak* (2:4).

11 Narrated by Hunād in *al-Zuhd* (489).

12 Narrated by al-Ḥākim in *al-Mustadrak* (2:4), and by Ibn Mājah (2144).

Abū Hurayra said, "The Messenger of God صَلَّىٱللَّهُعَلَيْهِوَسَلَّمَ said, 'O Abū Hurayra, if you become severely hungry, have a single piece of bread and a cup of water, and let [this] world go to perdition.'"[13]

Abū Hurayra رَضِيَٱللَّهُعَنْهُ said, "The Messenger of God صَلَّىٱللَّهُعَلَيْهِوَسَلَّمَ said, 'Be scrupulous, and you will be the most devoted of all in your worship. Be satisfied, and you will be the most thankful of all people. Love for other people what you love for yourself, and you will be a believer.'"[14]

The Messenger of God صَلَّىٱللَّهُعَلَيْهِوَسَلَّمَ forbade greed (*al-ṭamʿ*), as we read in the following account by Abū Ayyūb al-Anṣārī: "A certain desert Arab came to the Prophet صَلَّىٱللَّهُعَلَيْهِوَسَلَّمَ and said, 'O Messenger of God, grant me wise counsel in just a few words.' To this he صَلَّىٱللَّهُعَلَيْهِوَسَلَّمَ replied, 'When you pray, pray as though you were bidding farewell [to this world], say nothing you would have to apologize for the following day, and cling to no hope for what others possess.'"[15]

> ʿAwf b. Mālik al-Ashjaʿī said:
>
> There were nine, eight, or seven of us in the presence of the Messenger of God صَلَّىٱللَّهُعَلَيْهِوَسَلَّمَ, and he said, "Won't you pledge allegiance to the Messenger of God?"
>
> And we replied, "Have we not pledged allegiance to 140
> you, O Messenger of God?"
>
> Then again he said, "Won't you pledge allegiance to the Messenger of God?"
>
> So we reached out and pledged allegiance to him.
>
> Then someone among us said, "We have now pledged allegiance to you, O Messenger of God. So, what vow shall we make to you?"
>
> And he replied, "To worship God, and not to associate any partner with Him; to perform the five daily prayers; to hear and obey, and" – here he added under his breath – "not to ask anything of other people."

13 Narrated by al-Bayhaqī in *al-Shuʿab* (9881).

14 Narrated by Ibn Mājah (4217) and by al-Bayhaqī in *al-Shuʿab* (5366).

15 Narrated by Ibn Mājah (4171).

To this [ʿAwf] added, "Among these people were individuals who, if a whip fell out of their hand, they would not ask anyone to hand it to them [not wanting to ask anything of another person]."[16]

***

Traditions

ʿUmar رَضِيَ ٱللَّهُ عَنْهُ said, "Greed (*al-ṭamʿ*) is poverty (*faqr*), while relinquishing all hope [of what others can do for us] (*al-yaʾs*) is affluence (*ghinā*). Those who place no hope in what other people possess have ceased to need them."[17]

A certain sage was once asked, "What is affluence?" And he said, "It is to have few wishes, and to be content with whatever is enough for you."[18]

On this theme the following verses have been composed:[19]

> Life consists in hours that pass
> And days that repeat themselves.
>
> Be content with your lot and you will be satisfied
> Abandon your passions, and you will be free.
>
> Many a death has been occasioned
> By gold, sapphires, and pearls.

141 Muḥammad b. Wāsiʿ used to moisten dry bread with water and eat it, saying, "Whoever is satisfied with this will need no one."[20]

Sufyān said, "The best of what you have in [this] world is that through which you have not been tested. And the best things through which to be tested are those that leave your possession."[21]

---

16 Narrated by Muslim (1043), Abū Dāwūd (1642), and al-Nasāʾī (1:229).

17 Narrated by Ibn al-Mubārak in *al-Zuhd* (631).

18 Narrated by Abū Bakr al-Shāshī in his *Fawāʾid* (6).

19 See the commentary on *Nahj al-Balāgha* [The way of eloquence] (19:163).

20 Abū Nuʿaym related in *al-Ḥilya* (353) that Muḥammad b. Wāsiʿ was asked to serve as a judge, but he declined. When his wife chastised him for his refusal, saying, "You've got children, and you're needy!" he replied, "As long as you see me willing to put up with meals of vinegar and greens, don't expect me to do such a thing."

21 Narrated by Ibn al-Mubārak in *al-Zuhd* (541), and by Abū Nuʿaym in *al-Ḥilya* (7:21) with a similar wording.

Ibn Masʿūd رَضِيَ ٱللَّهُ عَنْهُ said, "Not a day goes by without an angel crying out, 'O son of Adam! A little that will suffice you is better than a lot that will rule over you like a tyrant.'"[22]

Shumayṭ b. ʿAjlān once said, "O son of Adam, your belly is only a hand span in diameter. So why allow it to send you into the fire?"[23]

A sage was once asked, "Of what does your wealth consist?" To which he replied, "Beautifying myself externally, practicing frugality internally, and not hoping for what others possess."

It has been narrated that God عَزَّ وَجَلَّ said, "O son of Adam, if the whole world were yours, all you would have of it is your daily sustenance (*al-qūt*). So, if I give you from [this world] your daily sustenance, and make others accountable for [the excess they receive from this world], I have been good to you."

Ibn Masʿūd said, "If one of you asks for something, let him 142
ask for it politely. Let none of you approach another in a harsh or demanding manner, wearing him down. For each is bound to receive what has been allotted to him, or what has been foreordained for his sustenance."[24]

A certain Umayyad wrote to Abū Ḥāzim urging him to ask him for whatever he needed. So, he [Abū Ḥāzim] wrote in reply, "I have brought my needs before my Master. Whatever He has given me of [those needs], I will accept, and whatever He has withheld from me, I will be satisfied without."[25]

A certain sage was asked, "What is the most pleasing thing for a judicious person? And what is most helpful in driving away sorrow?" He replied, "Most pleasing to a judicious person are the righteous works he has performed, and most helpful in driving away sorrow is contentment (*al-riḍā*) with what fate has decreed."[26]

A certain wise man said, "I have found that the one who remains distressed for the longest time is the envious; the one who most enjoys his life is the satisfied; the one most patient in hardship is the covetous if he aspires for more; the one who lives most simply

---

22 This is how the text reads in *al-Qūt* and *Itḥāf* (8:161).

23 This is how the text reads in *al-Qūt* and *Itḥāf* (8:161).

24 Narrated by al-Bukhārī in *al-Adab al-Mufrad* (779).

25 Narrated by Abū Nuʿaym in *al-Ḥilya* (3:237).

26 Transmitted by the author of *al-Qūt*. See *Itḥāf* (8:162).

is he who most rejects [this] world; and the most regretful is the scholar guilty of neglect."

Concerning this point the following verses have been composed:[27]

Peace belongs to youths who know
their Lord will their sustenance bestow.

143 Their honor ever unsullied.
Their countenances aglow,

Those who know satisfaction
Shall surely fear no woe.

The following verses were also composed:[28]

How long will I wander from place to place,
In a never-ending quest

Homeless, ever in exile
My loved ones far from my breast

For a time in the East, for a time in the West
So covetous that I think not of death

Were I satisfied, my sustenance would reach me
For affluence is satisfaction, not what I possess.[29]

ʿUmar رَضِيَ اللَّهُ عَنْهُ once said, "Shall I tell you what of God's عَزَّ وَجَلَّ wealth I view as lawful? Two garments, one for winter and one for summer, and something to cover my back for my *hajj* and my *ʿumra*. My daily sustenance beyond this would be like that of a man of Quraysh, neither the most wealthy nor the most destitute. Yet by God, I am not certain whether [even] this is lawful or not."[30] It was as though

---

27 The verses of poetry are from al-ʿAṭwī's *dīwān* (84) (*al-Mawrid* magazine, Volume 1, 1391 AH/1971 CE, Issues 1 and 2), and the third in *Bahjat al-Majālis* [The beauty of literary gatherings] (3:309).

28 These verses have been attributed to Ibn al-ʿAtāhiya in his *dīwān* (628), and to Kulthūm al-ʿItābī. See *al-ʿIqd al-Farīd* [The rare necklace] (3:208-209).

29 Narrated by al-Dīnawarī in *al-Mujālasa wa-jawhar al-ʿilm* [Scholarly gatherings and the essence of knowledge] (371), which was purportedly composed by al-Maʾmūn while he was on his way back to Tarsus.

30 Narrated by Zanjawayh in *al-Amwāl* [Money] (989), and Ibn ʿAsākir in *Tārīkh Dimashq* (44:270).

he suspected that even this modest provision was more than the sufficiency with which he ought to be satisfied.

Reprimanding a brother for his covetousness, one desert Arab said, "Brother, you are both a seeker and that which is sought. You 144
are sought by that which you cannot avoid [that is, death], while you seek that which has already been guaranteed to you [that is, your sustenance]. It is as though you are able to visualize what you have been deprived of, while being removed from what you are already swimming in. My brother, it is as though you had never seen a covetous person who remains deprived, or an abstemious person (*zāhid*) who has been provided with the sustenance he needs."[31]

On this topic, the following verses were composed:[32]

> Wealth only draws you covetously more to [this] world
> as though you will never see death.
>
> Will you ever, in pursuit of a goal
> say, "Enough! I have become content"?

Al-Shaʿbī related:

> Once upon a time, a man captured a lark.
>
> "What are you going to do with me?" asked the lark.
>
> "I'm going to slaughter you and eat you," the man replied.
>
> "I tell you truly," the lark said, "I will not satisfy your cravings for meat, nor anyone's hunger. However, I will teach you three qualities that will do you more good than it would to eat me. One of them, I will teach you while I'm in your hand. The second, I will teach you from the tree. And the third, I will teach you from the mountain."
>
> "Teach me the first one," [the man] said.
>
> "Do not lament what has passed you by," she said.
>
> Then he let her go.
>
> Once the lark was in the tree, [the man] said, "Teach me the second one."
>
> And the lark said, "Do not believe in the existence of something that could never be."

---

31 Narrated by Ibn Abī al-Dunyā in *al-Zuhd* (314).

32 From the *dīwān* of Maḥmūd al-Warrāq (89).

> Then she flew up and went onto the mountain and said, "You poor man, if you slaughtered me, you would find two pearls in my craw, each of them weighing 20 miskals."[33] Upon hearing this, the man bit his lip and lamented.
>
> "Teach me the third one," he said.
>
> "How do you expect me to teach you the third one when
> you've already forgotten the first two?" the lark rejoined.
> "Did I not tell you to not lament what has passed you by?
> And to not believe in the existence of something that could
> 145 never be? My flesh, my blood and my feathers all together
> weigh less than 20 miskals. So how could there be two pearls
> in my craw, each of them weighing 20 miskals?"
>
> Then she took flight and was gone."[34]

This story exemplifies human beings' excessive greed (*ṭamᶜ*), which so blinds them from perceiving reality that they consider things to exist that, in fact, have no existence.

Ibn al-Sammāk said, "Hope [for this world] is a tether that binds your heart, and a shackle about your leg. Remove the hope from your heart, and the shackle will fall from your leg."[35]

> Abū Muḥammad al-Yazīdī said:
>
> I went in to see [Hārūn] al-Rashīd, and found him looking at a piece of paper on which gold letters had been penned. When he saw me, he smiled.
>
> I said, "Hopefully there are glad tidings, may God prosper the Commander of the Faithful."
>
> He replied, 'Yes. I found these two verses of poetry in Banī Umayya's storehouses, and I found them beautiful and edifying. I've also added a third verse of my own."
>
> Then he recited to me:[36]

---

33 Trans.: A *miskal* is a unit of weight in the Islamic world, usually taken as equivalent to 4.25 grams, and used especially to weigh precious metals, such as gold, and other commodities, such as saffron.

34 Narrated by Abū Nuᶜaym in *al-Ḥilya* (4:316).

35 Narrated by Ibn Ḥibbān in *Rawḍat al-ᶜUqalāʾ* [Garden of the wise] (143).

36 See *Bahjat al-Majālis* (3:310) and *Mukhtaṣar Tārīkh Dimashq* [An abridged history of Damascus] (27:25).

> If the door to a need closes,
> Another may open before you.
>
> It will suffice to fill your belly in part,
> And avoiding the shameful will protect you.
>
> Squander not your honor, shun acts of disobedience,
> And their punishment will avoid you."

ʿAbdallāh b. Sallām said to Kaʿb, "What causes scholars to lose their knowledge after they comprehended and understood it?" And he replied, "Greed (*al-ṭamʿ*), gluttony of soul, and seeking after things."[37]

> A man once said to al-Fuḍayl, "Explain to me what 146
> Kaʿb said."
>
> [Al-Fuḍayl] replied, "When someone craves something and seeks it out, it will cause him to lose his religion. As for the gluttonous person, he desires this and that, not wanting anything to pass him by. [If you are of this type,] you will feel this need and that need. And if someone meets your need, he will insert a ring in your nose and lead you wherever he wants you to go. In so doing, he gains power over you. Then, it is due to your love for [this] world that when you pass him, you greet him, and if he falls ill, you pay him a visit. You do not greet him for the sake of God عَزَّوَجَلَّ, nor do you visit him for the sake of God عَزَّوَجَلَّ. If you had no need for [this person], it would be better for you."
>
> Then he added, "Indeed, this would be better for you than a hundred *ḥadīth*s on the authority of so-and-so and so-and-so."[38]

A certain sage once said, "One of the peculiar things about human beings is that if they were invited to prolong their days in [this] world indefinitely, they would have no more urge to accumulate than they do when their days on earth are numbered and with the expectation that their lives will come to an end."[39]

37 Narrated by Ibn ʿAsākir in *Tārīkh Dimashq* (50:171).

38 Narrated, with the previous report, by al-Qāḍī ʿIyāḍ in *al-Ilmāʿ* (194).

39 Sourced by Ibn Abī al-Dunyā. See *Itḥāf* (9:164).

ʿAbd al-Wāḥid b. Zayd said, "I once went to see a monk and I asked him, 'Where do you get food to eat?' And he said, 'From the threshing floor of the Subtle, the Aware (*al-laṭīf al-khabīr*). He who created the hand mill will supply it with the wheat.' Then he pointed to the 'hand mills' of his molar teeth."[40] Glory be to the Almighty, the Aware.

***

40 Sourced by Ibn Abī al-Dunyā. See *Itḥāf* (9:164). It was also narrated by Ibn ʿAsākir in *Tārīkh Dimashq* (6:11) as part of a long report, but on the authority of al-Salīṭ b. Sabīʿ.

5

An Elucidation of the Remedy for Covetousness (*al-ḥirṣ*) and Greed (*al-ṭamʿ*), and of the Medicine by which One Attains the Attribute of Satisfaction (*al-qanāʿa*) 147

KNOW that this medicine consists of three main pillars: patience, knowledge, and action. Moreover, those [three pillars] involve five concerns:

The first [of these concerns], namely, action, entails moderation in one's lifestyle, and care and gentleness (*rifq*) in [one's approach to] spending. Whoever wishes to experience the glory of satisfaction must, so far as he is able, keep his expenses to a minimum, keeping away from that which he does not need. Whoever incurs major expenses and spends freely will not be able to experience satisfaction. Whoever is alone should satisfy himself with a single, coarse garment and be satisfied with whatever food is available. He should consume as few rich foods as possible, and accustom himself to this regimen. If he has children, he should accustom each of them to this humble fare. This way of life can be mastered with minimal effort, and in this way [a person] can be general [that is, not highly specific and rarified] in what he seeks to acquire.

A frugal lifestyle is the foundation of satisfaction, and by this we mean: care and gentleness in [one's approach to] spending and an abandonment of folly in [spending].

The Messenger of God صَلَّىٱللَّهُعَلَيْهِوَسَلَّمَ said, "God loves gentleness (*rifq*) in all things."[1]

---

1 Narrated by al-Bukhārī (6024) and Muslim (2165).

148 He صَلَّىٱللَّهُعَلَيْهِوَسَلَّمَ also said, "Whoever is moderate (*iqtaṣada*) will never suffer poverty."[2]

He صَلَّىٱللَّهُعَلَيْهِوَسَلَّمَ said, "There are three things that will rescue you [from the fire]: the fear of God in private and in public, frugality (*al-qasd*) in both poverty and affluence; and fairness in both contentment and anger."[3]

A man once saw Abū l-Dardāʾ gleaning grain from the earth, and said, "Your gentleness in your lifestyle is a sign of your understanding."[4]

Ibn ʿAbbās said, "The Prophet صَلَّىٱللَّهُعَلَيْهِوَسَلَّمَ once said, 'Moderation (*iqtiṣād*), good manners, and right guidance constitute one of the twenty-odd parts of prophethood.'"[5]

One report reads, "Management (*al-tadbīr*) is half of living."[6]

He صَلَّىٱللَّهُعَلَيْهِوَسَلَّمَ said, "Whoever is moderate, God will make rich;
149 whoever is wasteful, God will make poor; and whoever remembers
God عَزَّوَجَلَّ, God will love."[7]

He صَلَّىٱللَّهُعَلَيْهِوَسَلَّمَ said, "If you want something, proceed deliberately until God provides you with relief, and a way out [of your difficulty]."[8] Deliberateness (*al-tuʾada*) in relation to one's spending is one of the most important things [in life].

***

The second [concern] is that whoever has enough to meet his needs in the present, he need not be overly distraught over the future. This is made all the easier by the refusal to place hope [in this world], and by the certainty that he is bound to receive the sustenance which has been foreordained for him, even if he does not strongly covet it. After

2 Narrated by Aḥmad in *al-Musnad* (1:447), by Ibn Abī al-Dunyā in *Iṣlāḥ al-Māl* [The correct management of wealth] (348), and by al-Ṭabarānī in *al-Kabīr* (10:108).

3 Narrated by al-Kharāʾiṭī in *Iʿtilāl al-qulūb* [The malady of hearts] (102), by Abū Nuʿaym in *al-Ḥilya* (2:343), and by al-Bayhaqī in *al-Shuʿab* (731).

4 Narrated by al-Bayhaqī in *al-Shuʿab* (6144, 6145).

5 Narrated by Abū Dāwūd (4776) with a different order, and by al-Tirmidhī (2010), who replaced *al-hadī al-ṣāliḥ* (right guidance) with *al-tuʾada* (deliberateness or prudence).

6 Narrated by al-Quḍāʿī in *Musnad al-Shihāb* (32) and by al-Daylamī in *Musnad al-Firdaws* (3421).

7 Narrated by Ibn Abī Shayba in *al-Muṣannaf* (25821) and by al-Bukhārī in *al-Adab al-Mufrad* (888).

8 Narrated in its entirety by Ibn Abī al-Dunyā in *Iṣlāḥ al-Māl* (328).

all, intense covetousness is not what causes [a person] to receive the sustenance they need. Rather, he must trust in the promise of God سُبْحَانَهُ وَتَعَالَى, who says عَزَّ وَجَلَّ, *And there is no creature on earth but that upon God is its provision* [Q. 11:6]. However, *Satan threatens you with poverty and orders you to immorality* [Q. 2:268], saying, "Unless you strive mightily to amass stores [of wealth], you may fall ill and be afflicted with incapacity, so you will be forced to beg and suffer the resulting humiliation." And so [a person] spends his life anxiously seeking [more and more] out of fear of suffering. Meanwhile, [Satan] laughs at him for the suffering he endures in the present while, at the same time, he grows heedless of God عَزَّ وَجَلَّ—all due to some hypothetical future hardship that may never come to pass.

Indeed, al-Mutanabbī said,

> Those who spend the hours amassing wealth
> for fear of poverty, do [themselves] act out of poverty.[9]

Khālid's two sons went in to see the Messenger of God صَلَّى ٱللَّهُ عَلَيْهِ وَسَلَّمَ, 150
and he said to them, "Despair not of your daily sustenance so long as you have life within you.[10] When our mothers bear us, we are red-skinned and hairless creatures; then God سُبْحَانَهُ وَتَعَالَى provides our sustenance."[11]

The Messenger of God صَلَّى ٱللَّهُ عَلَيْهِ وَسَلَّمَ went to see Ibn Masʿūd at a time when the latter was feeling sad. So he said to him, "Do not worry excessively. That which is foreordained will be. And that which is destined to be provided for you will come."[12]

He صَلَّى ٱللَّهُ عَلَيْهِ وَسَلَّمَ said, "Listen, O people. Be moderate in what you seek to acquire, for no one can obtain more than what has been written for him, nor will anyone depart from [this] world until he receives what is written for him therein, no matter what."[13]

---

9 From the *dīwān* of al-Mutanabbī with commentary by al-ʿAkbarī (2:150).

10 Trans.: That is, so long as you live.

11 Narrated by Ibn Mājah (4165) and by al-Ṭabarānī in *al-Kabīr* (4:7). The two sons of Khālid to whom reference is made here are Ḥabba and Sawdāʾ رَضِيَ ٱللَّهُ عَنْهُمَا.

12 Narrated by Ibn Abī al-Dunyā in *al-Faraj baʿd al-Shidda* [Relief after affliction] (19), by Abū Nuʿaym in *Maʿrifat al-Ṣaḥāba* [Knowledge of the companions] (2:944), and by al-Bayhaqī in *al-Shuʿab* (1144).

13 Al-Ḥākim narrated a similar account in *al-Mustadrak* (2:4).

The only thing that will free us from covetousness is confidence in God's سُبْحَانَهُ وَتَعَالَىٰ management in supplying all His servants' needs, and [confidence] that this sustenance is bound to come if we are general in what we seek [to acquire]. In fact, we should know that our sustenance will come primarily whence we know not. God سُبْحَانَهُ وَتَعَالَىٰ says, *And whoever fears God - He will make for him a way out, and will provide for him from where he does not expect. And whoever relies upon God - then He is sufficient for him. Indeed, God will accomplish His purpose. God has already set for everything a [decreed] extent* [Q. 65:2-3]. Therefore, if a door through which we had awaited our sustenance closes, our hearts should not be troubled on this account.

151 The Messenger of God صَلَّى ٱللَّهُ عَلَيْهِ وَسَلَّمَ said, "God will always provide for His believing servant whence he does not expect it."[14]

Sufyān said, "Fear God, for never have I seen a God-fearing person in need."[15] In other words, God will not leave anyone who fears Him deprived of what he needs. Rather, God will place a burden on Muslims' hearts to provide for this person's sustenance.[16]

> Al-Mufaḍḍal al-Ḍabbī said:
>
> I once asked a desert Arab, "From where do you get what you need to live?"
>
> "From the pilgrims," he replied.
>
> "And when they leave?" I queried.
>
> In response, he wept and said, "If we lived only on sources we knew from whence they came, we would not survive."[17]

---

14 Narrated by Ibn Ḥibbān in *al-Majrūḥin* [Rejected *ḥadīth* transmitters] (1:161), by al-Quḍāʿī in *Musnad al-Shihāb* (585), and by al-Bayhaqī in *al-Shuʿab* (1152).

15 In his *Itḥāf* (8:168), al-Ḥāfiẓ al-Zabīdī said, "This was presented by the author of *al-Ḥilya* as though he had inferred it from the words of God سُبْحَانَهُ وَتَعَالَىٰ, *And whoever fears God - He will make for him a way out, and will provide for him from where he does not expect. And whoever relies upon God - then He is sufficient for him. Indeed, God will accomplish His purpose. God has already set for everything a* [*decreed*] *extent* [Q. 65:2-3], the implication being that when we fear God, it is inconceivable that we would be needy.

16 In other words, this will happen without a command from another human being, and without the needy person's having asked for help. See *Itḥāf* (8:168).

17 Narrated by Ibn ʿAsākir in *Tārīkh Dimashq* (56:248).

Abū Ḥāzim رَضِيَ اللَّهُ عَنْهُ said, "I have found in [this] world two kinds of things. One of these belongs to me; however, I could not force it to come before its time, even if I sought it with the power of the heavens and the earth. The other thing belongs to someone else; hence, I have not obtained it in the past, nor would I hope to obtain it in the future. That which belongs to someone else could never be mine, just as that which belongs to me could never belong to someone else. So why should I fritter my life away in pursuit of either of them?"[18]

This is a medicine that comes from spiritual knowledge which 152
we must have in order to ward off Satan's attempts to frighten us with the spectre of poverty.

***

The third [concern] is for [the person] to know the glory of self-sufficiency that satisfaction brings, and what abasement and humiliation are caused by covetousness and greed (*al-ṭamʿ*). When he realizes these things, it causes him to desire satisfaction. For in covetousness, one is never free of weariness; and in greed, one is never free of disgrace. Whereas the only pain occasioned by satisfaction is that of the patience required to resist one's cravings and preferences. This type of pain is known only to God, and yields a reward in the hereafter.

And that is of what is visible to other people's eyes, which includes the evil consequences of a deed, and misdeeds themselves. Furthermore, they deprive themselves of inner glory and the ability to surrender to the truth. For the greater the greed and covetousness, the more [a person] needs other people, as a result of which he is not in a position to exhort them to embrace the truth. Instead, he finds himself obliged to engage in flattery, which is perilous to his *dīn*. He who does not value inner glory over the cravings of the belly is weak of intellect and even weaker of faith.

As the Messenger of God صَلَّى اللَّهُ عَلَيْهِ وَسَلَّمَ said, "The glory of believers consists in their ability to do without other people."[19]

18 Narrated by Abū Nuʿaym in *al-Ḥilya* (3:237), and by al-Bayhaqī in *al-Shuʿab* (1240).

19 Narrated by al-Ṭabarānī in *al-Awsaṭ* (4290), and by Abū Nuʿaym in *al-Ḥilya* (3:253) on the authority of Sahl b. Saʿd رَضِيَ اللَّهُ عَنْهُ, who said, "Gabriel came to the Prophet صَلَّى اللَّهُ عَلَيْهِ وَسَلَّمَ and said, 'O Muḥammad, however long you live, you are bound to die.

In satisfaction there is freedom and glory. Therefore, it has been
153 said, "When you do not need another, you are his equal; when you need another, you are his captive; and when you do good for another, you are his leader (*amīr*)."[20]

***

The fourth [concern] is that one should give careful thought to the lives of luxury lived by Jews and Christians and the most contemptible of people, including the fools among the Kurds[21] and the uncivilized among the desert Arabs,[22] and whoever has neither religion nor good sense. Then one should turn one's thoughts to the lives lived by the prophets and saints, and the paths trodden by the rightly guided caliphs, as well as the ways of the Prophet's Companions and their Successors. One should pay attention to the accounts passed down about them and study their states. Having done so, one has a choice to make, between emulating the most despicable of people, and following in the footsteps of those who were the most honored of all human beings by God عَزَّوَجَلَّ, until one finds it easy to have patience with little and satisfaction with that which [comes with] ease. For if someone indulges his belly, the donkey will outdo him; if he succumbs to all his sexual urges, swine will hold a higher rank on the scale; and if he sports elegant clothing and purebred horses, there will be Jews[23] who outshine him. But if we satisfy ourselves with little and are content by it, no one will occupy a rank higher than ours but the prophets and saints.

Whatever you do, you will be rewarded for it; whoever you love, you are bound to part. Know that the believer's honor lies in rising by night to worship, and that his strength lies in his autonomy from other people.'"

20 Narrated by Ibn ʿAsākir in *Tārīkh Dimashq* (67:184) on the authority of Abū Muḥammad al-Anṣārī, who is said to have read these words on a rock in Jerusalem.

21 Eds.: In the time of the author, this was a euphemism for isolated mountain dwellers who are hostile to people "other" than them.

22 Eds.: Similarly, in the time of the author, this was a euphemism for isolated dwellers of a harsh environment who are hostile to people "other" than them. In all references to a community of people, it is the unfaithful and corrupt actions and behaviors among these people observed in the time of the author which the author is referencing, never an ethnicity or religious group as a whole.

23 Eds.: Here meaning someone belonging to a wealthy community. See previous footnote.

***

The fifth [concern] is to understand the dangers that accompany the accumulation of money as we mentioned in our discussion of the harms of wealth, including the fear of theft, of being looted, and of destruction and loss. Similarly, [we need to see] that not possessing wealth brings a sense of security and spaciousness. We should contemplate the harms of wealth, one of which is that it bars the entrance of the garden [to a person] for as much as five hundred 154
years. And if [a person] is not content with that which meets his needs, he will join the ranks of the affluent, being expelled from the ranks of the poor [who will be welcomed immediately into the garden]. He can avoid this fate by looking always at those who are of lesser rank than he in [this] world, not at those who are above him. Satan is perpetually urging us to look at those who are above us in [this] world, saying, "Why don't you seek more, as the owners of wealth live in luxury, enjoying all manner of food, drink, and raiment?" In the [realm of the] *dīn*, by contrast, he urges us to look at those who are below us, saying, "Why should you place restrictions on yourself and fear God, when so-and-so is more knowledgeable than you are, yet does not fear God? Everyone [around you] is preoccupied with [the search for] creature comforts. Why should you want to be any different from them?"

Abū Dharr رَضِيَ ٱللَّهُ عَنْهُ once said, "My dear friend صَلَّى ٱللَّهُ عَلَيْهِ وَسَلَّمَ instructed me to look at those who are below me, not at those who are above me,"[24] that is, in [this] world.

Abū Hurayra said, "The Messenger of God صَلَّى ٱللَّهُ عَلَيْهِ وَسَلَّمَ said, 'If any of you looks at others who have been blessed with more wealth and beauty, let him look instead at those who have been blessed with less.'"[25]

In these ways, we can acquire the disposition of satisfaction. The foundation of this state is patience and few expectations. We should know that the practice of patience in [this] world is for a short time only, [in exchange] for an eternity of bliss. [The situation] can be likened to that of a sick person who endures the bitterness of medicine out of his strong desire for the possibility healing.

---

24 Narrated by Aḥmad in *al-Musnad* (5:159), and by Ibn Ḥibbān in his *Ṣaḥīḥ* (449).

25 Narrated by al-Bukhārī (6490) and Muslim (2963).

6

155 ## An Elucidation of the Virtue of Generosity (*al-sakhāʾ*)

KNOW that if wealth is lacking, the state of the servant must demonstrate satisfaction (*al-qanāʿa*) and little covetousness. Whereas if it is present, his state should demonstrate altruism (*al-īthār*) and generosity (*al-sakhāʾ*), a willingness to do good for others, and he should avoid avarice (*al-shuḥḥ*) and miserliness (*al-bukhl*). For generosity is one of the virtues of the prophets عَلَيْهِمُ ٱلسَّلَامُ. It is also one of the foundations of salvation. Of it the Prophet صَلَّى ٱللَّٰهُ عَلَيْهِ وَسَلَّمَ once said, "Generosity is from the trees of the [heavenly] garden, the branches of which hang down to earth. Whoever takes hold of one of its branches, that branch will lead him to the garden."[1]

Jābir said, "The Messenger of God صَلَّى ٱللَّٰهُ عَلَيْهِ وَسَلَّمَ said: Gabriel عَلَيْهِ ٱلسَّلَامُ said: God سُبْحَانَهُ وَتَعَالَىٰ said, 'This is a *dīn* which I have chosen for myself, but it can only be practiced correctly through generosity and beauty of character (*ḥusn al-khalq*). So honor [this religion] with them to the extent that you are able.'"[2]

ʿĀʾisha the Righteous رَضِيَ ٱللَّٰهُ عَنْهَا said, "The Messenger of God
156 صَلَّى ٱللَّٰهُ عَلَيْهِ وَسَلَّمَ said, 'God سُبْحَانَهُ وَتَعَالَىٰ has created every one of His

1 Narrated by Ibn ʿAdī in *al-Kāmil* (1:235), by Abū Nuʿaym in *al-Ḥilya* (7:92), and by al-Kharkūshī in *Tahdhīb al-Asrār* [A brief compendium of mysteries] (421), to be quoted in full below.

2 Or: "Therefore, honor it with them so long as you are associated with it." Narrated by al-Kharāʾiṭī in *Makārim al-Akhlāq* [Refined morals] (39, 559), by al-Ṭabarānī in *al-Awsaṭ* (8915), and by al-Bayhaqī in *al-Shuʿab* (10366). The same wording is given for both versions of it by al-Kharkūshi in *Tahdhīb al-Asrār* (422).

saints with a natural disposition for generosity and beauty of character.'"[3]

According to Jābir, someone once said, "O Messenger of God, which are the best of all virtues?" And he replied, "Patience and magnanimity (*al-sabr wa-l-samāḥa*)."[4]

According to ʿAbdallāh b. ʿAmr, the Messenger of God صَلَّى ٱللَّهُ عَلَيْهِ وَسَلَّمَ said, "There are two character traits which God عَزَّ وَجَلَّ loves, and two character traits which God عَزَّ وَجَلَّ abhors. The two which He عَزَّ وَجَلَّ loves are beauty of character and generosity, while the two which He عَزَّ وَجَلَّ abhors are depraved character and miserliness. If God wishes to bless [one of His] servants, He uses him to meet people's needs."[5]

Al-Miqdām b. Shurayḥ related on the authority of his father that his grandfather had said, "O Messenger of God, guide me to an action that will usher me into the garden." And he replied, "Some of the actions that bring forgiveness are sharing food, spreading peace, and beauty of speech (*ḥusn al-kalām*)."[6]

Abū Hurayra رَضِيَ ٱللَّهُ عَنْهُ said, "The Messenger of God صَلَّى ٱللَّهُ عَلَيْهِ وَسَلَّمَ once said, 'Generosity (*al-sakhā᾿*) is a tree in the garden. If a generous person takes one of its branches, that branch will not let go of him 157
until it has ushered him into the garden. As for avarice (*al-shuḥḥ*), it is a tree in the fire. If an avaricious person takes hold of one of its branches, that branch will not let go of him until it has ushered him into the fire.'"[7]

Abū Saʿīd al-Khudrī said, "The Messenger of God صَلَّى ٱللَّهُ عَلَيْهِ وَسَلَّمَ said, 'God سُبْحَانَهُ وَتَعَالَىٰ says, "Seek favor from the merciful of My

---

3 This *ḥadīth* is mentioned by al-Ḥakīm al-Tirmidhī in *Nawādir al-Uṣūl fī ma'rifat aḥadīth al-rasūl* [The unique principles that emerge from the knowledge of the traditions of the Messenger] (105), by al-Kharkūshī in *Tahdhīb al-Asrār* (422), and by al-Daylamī in *Musnad al-Firdaws* [a Sunni *ḥadīth* collection] (6228).

4 Narrated by Ibn Abī Shayba in *al-Muṣannaf* (31032), by Abū Yaʿlā in his *Musnad* (1854), and by Aḥmad in his *Musnad* (4:385) from a *ḥadīth* of ʿAmr b. ʿAnbasa رَضِيَ ٱللَّهُ عَنْهُ.

5 Narrated by al-Bayhaqī in *al-Shuʿab* (7253) and by al-Daylamī in *Musnad al-Firdaws* (2989).

6 Narrated by al-Ṭabarānī in *al-Kabīr* (22:180) in two different versions which he has combined here. The version included by al-Ghazālī is also the same as that included by al-Kharkūshī in *Tahdhīb al-Asrār* (423).

7 Narrated by al-Bayhaqī in *al-Shuʿab* (10377).

servants, and you will live under their protection. For I have placed my mercy within them. Ask nothing from the hard-hearted, for in them have I placed my wrath.'""[8]

Ibn ʿAbbās said, "The Messenger of God صَلَّى ٱللَّهُ عَلَيْهِ وَسَلَّمَ said, 'Overlook the sins of the generous, for God takes them by the hand whenever they stumble.'"[9]

Ibn Mas'ūd said, "The Messenger of God صَلَّى ٱللَّهُ عَلَيْهِ وَسَلَّمَ said, 'Sustenance will reach those who feed the hungry more quickly than the knife reaches the camel's hump, and God سُبْحَانَهُ وَتَعَالَىٰ will boast to the angels عَلَيْهِمُ ٱلسَّلَامُ about those who have fed the hungry.'"[10]

158 He صَلَّى ٱللَّهُ عَلَيْهِ وَسَلَّمَ said, "God is openhanded (*jawād*), and loves openhandedness (*al-jūd*). Similarly, God loves refined character, and abhors inferior behavior."[11]

Anas رَضِيَ ٱللَّهُ عَنْهُ said, "Never was the Messenger of God صَلَّى ٱللَّهُ عَلَيْهِ وَسَلَّمَ asked for anything [as proof] of Islam's truth but that he gave it. Thus, a man once came to him and asked him [for something], whereupon he ordered that the man be given numerous ewes between two mountains that had been designated as alms. The man then went back to his people, saying, 'Embrace Islam, O people, for Muḥammad gives with the liberality of one who has no fear of poverty.'"[12]

Ibn ʿUmar رَضِيَ ٱللَّهُ عَنْهُمَا said, "The Messenger of God صَلَّى ٱللَّهُ عَلَيْهِ وَسَلَّمَ said, 'God has servants on whom He bestows blessings in order to benefit other servants [of God]. If they are miserly with these blessings

---

8 Narrated by al-Kharāʾiṭī in *Makārim al-Akhlāq* (568), by Ibn Ḥibbān in *al-Majrūḥīn* (2:299), by al-Ṭabarānī in *al-Awsaṭ* (4714), and by al-Quḍāʿī in *Musnad al-Shihāb* (700).

9 Narrated by al-Ṭabarānī in *al-Awsaṭ* (5706); by Abū Nuʿaym in *al-Ḥilya* (9:397 and 4:108, the latter instance being from the *ḥadīth* of Ibn Masʿūd رَضِيَ ٱللَّهُ عَنْهُ); and by al-Bayhaqī in *al-Shuʿab* (10369).

10 This is how it reads in al-Kharkūshī's *Tahdhīb al-Asrār* (424), while Ibn Mājah (3356, 3357) narrated from a *ḥadīth* of Anas and Ibn ʿAbbās رَضِيَ ٱللَّهُ عَنْهُمَا that, "Blessing will reach the household where food is eaten—or provided—more rapidly than the knife blade reaches the camel's hump." A similar version was narrated here by al-Rāfiʿī in *Tārīkh Qazwīn* (4:120) from the *ḥadīth* of Jābir رَضِيَ ٱللَّهُ عَنْهُ.

11 Narrated by al-Kharāʾiṭī in *Makārim al-Akhlāq* (572) on the authority of Ṭalḥa b. ʿUbaydallāh b. Kurayz, omitting the name of the Companion from the *isnād*; it was narrated by Ibn Ḥibbān in *Rawḍat al-ʿUqalāʾ* (16), and by al-Ṭabarānī in *al-Kabīr* (6:181) from a *ḥadīth* of Sahl b. Saʿdallāh رَضِيَ ٱللَّهُ عَنْهُ. Some of it was cited previously.

12 Narrated by Muslim (2312).

which are bestowed upon servants [of God], God عَزَّوَجَلَّ will take these blessings away from them and give these [blessings] to others.'"[13]

It was related by al-Hilālī:

> Captives from the tribe of Banū al-ʿAnbar were brought to the Messenger of God صَلَّىٱللَّهُعَلَيْهِوَسَلَّمَ, who ordered them all killed except for one man.
>
> Seeing this, ʿAlī b. Abī Ṭālib رَضِيَٱللَّهُعَنْهُ said, "O Messenger of God, the Lord is one, the *dīn* is one, and the crime is one. So why would you spare this one person out of all the rest?"
>
> In response, he صَلَّىٱللَّهُعَلَيْهِوَسَلَّمَ said, "Gabriel came down 159
> and said to me, 'Kill those men, and spare this one. For God سُبْحَانَهُوَتَعَالَىٰ is rewarding him for some generosity within him.'"[14]

The Messenger of God صَلَّىٱللَّهُعَلَيْهِوَسَلَّمَ said, "To every thing there is a fruit, and the fruit of a good deed is the hastening of release."[15]

Nāfiʿ related that Ibn ʿUmar رَضِيَٱللَّهُعَنْهُمَا had said, "The Messenger of God صَلَّىٱللَّهُعَلَيْهِوَسَلَّمَ said, 'The food of the openhanded is a medicine (*dawāʾ*), while the food of the miserly is a disease (*dāʾ*).'"[16]

---

13 Narrated by Ibn Abī al-Dunyā in *Qaḍāʾ al-Ḥawāʾij* [The meeting of needs] (5), by al-Ṭabarānī in *al-Awsaṭ* (5158), and by Abū Nuʿaym in *al-Ḥilya* (6:115 and 10:215).

14 This is how it was narrated by al-Kharkūshī in *Tahdhīb al-Asrār* (425) with the following changes: al-Hilālī is replaced by al-Hudhalī, and the following text is added: "The captive asked, 'Why did I not join my companions?' And the reply came, 'God سُبْحَانَهُوَتَعَالَىٰ is rewarding you for some act of generosity on your part.' Thereupon, he embraced Islam and practiced it faithfully with the blessing of his acts of generosity." Al-Ḥāfiẓ al-ʿIrāqī states, "I have found no origin for it." See *Itḥāf* (8:175).

15 Al-Ḥāfiẓ al-Zabīdī states in his *Itḥāf* (8:175): "al-ʿIrāqī has said, 'I have found no origin for it.' However, I note that its meaning is correct. It is reflected in the saying, *immā niʿam ṣarīḥa wa illā murīḥa*…., that is to say, either explicitly grant the blessing sought, or explicitly refuse to do so, thus releasing the seeker from false hope. The report has dropped out of the printed version of *Tahdhīb al-Asrār* by al-Kharkūshī, although the context is there."

16 This is how the text reads in al-Dulaymī's *Musnad al-Firdaws* (3954). Al-Ḥāfiẓ al-ʿIrāqī said, "It was narrated by Ibn ʿAdī and al-Dāraquṭnī in *Gharāʾib Mālik* [a collection by Mālik b. Anas of *ḥadīths* classified as *gharīb*, or 'strange", for having been passed down by a single narrator], and by Abū ʿAlī al-Ṣūfī in his *ʿAwālī* [Trans.: Perhaps what is meant here is *ʿAwālī Musnad ʿAbd b. Ḥumayd* by Abū ʿĪsā al-Ṣūfī, d. 553/1139, where *ʿawālī* is the plural of *ʿālī*, referring to an *isnād* which is highly trustworthy], where he wrote, 'Its narrators are trustworthy, pious and learned.'

And he صَلَّىٱللَّهُعَلَيْهِوَسَلَّمَ said, "Whoever has received abundant blessing from God will be obliged to provide abundantly for other people. Whoever does not tolerate this obligation will cause this blessing to pass out of their hands."[17]

160 Jesus عَلَيْهِٱلسَّلَامُ said, "Accumulate in abundance that which will not be consumed by the fire." He was asked, "And what is that?" He replied, "Good deeds."[18]

ʿĀʾisha رَضِيَٱللَّهُعَنْهَا said, "The Messenger of God صَلَّىٱللَّهُعَلَيْهِوَسَلَّمَ said, 'The garden is the abode of the generous (*al-askhīyāʾ*).'"[19]

Abū Hurayra said, "The Messenger of God صَلَّىٱللَّهُعَلَيْهِوَسَلَّمَ said, 'The generous person is close to God, close to people, close to the garden, and far from the fire. As for the miserly person, he is far from God, far from people, far from the garden, and close to the fire. An ignorant, but generous person is dearer to God than a pious miser. The worst of all diseases is miserliness.'"[20]

The Messenger of God صَلَّىٱللَّهُعَلَيْهِوَسَلَّمَ said, "Do good deeds both for those who are worthy, and for those who are not. If those for whom you do good are worthy of it, you will have served the worthy. If not, you yourself will be among the worthy."[21]

161 And he صَلَّىٱللَّهُعَلَيْهِوَسَلَّمَ said, "The 'substitutes' (*budalāʾ*)[22] of my community [of Muslims] do not enter the garden based on ritual

---

Ibn al-Qaṭṭān said, 'They are well-known and trustworthy with the exception of Miqdām b. Dāwūd, as the scholars of Egypt have spoken [badly] of him.'" See *Itḥāf* (8:175).

17 Narrated by Ibn Abī al-Dunyā in *Qaḍāʾ al-Ḥawāʾij* (48) based on a *ḥadīth* of ʿĀʾisha رَضِيَٱللَّهُعَنْهَا, by Ibn ʿAdī in *al-Kāmil* (1:174), and by al-Quḍāʿī in *Musnad al-Shihāb* (798) based on a *ḥadīth* of Muʿādh b. Jabal رَضِيَٱللَّهُعَنْهُ.

18 This is how the text is cited by al-Kharkūshī in *Tahdhīb al-Asrār* (427) and by Abū Nuʿaym in *al-Ḥilya* (3:371) on the authority of al-Zuhrī.

19 Narrated by al-Kharāʾiṭī in *Makārim al-Akhlāq* (597), by Ibn Ḥibbān in *Kitāb al-Thiqāt* [The book of trustworthy narrators] (5:23), and by Ibn ʿAdī in *al-Kāmil* (1:187).

20 Narrated by al-Tirmidhī (1961) without the last sentence, and by al-Kharāʾiṭī in *Masāwiʾ al-Akhlāq* [Bad morals] (374).

21 Narrated by Abū Bakr al-Shāfiʿī in *al-Ghaylāniyāt* (78), by al-Jaṣṣāṣ in *Aḥkām al-Qurʾān* [Rulings of the Qurʾān (3:267), by al-Sulamī in *Ādāb al-Ṣuḥba* [The etiquette of companionship] (138), and by al-Dāraquṭnī in *al-ʿIlal al-wāridah fī al-aḥādīth* [Faulty *ḥadīths*] (3:107).

22 Trans.: The *budalāʾ*, or *abdāl* (plural of *badīl*), who belong to the fourth rank of Sufi saints, are not recognized by people in [this] world.

prayer or fasting. Rather, they enter it due to the generosity of their souls, the purity of their breasts (*al-ṣudūr*), and the sound counsel they give other Muslims."[23]

Abū Saʿīd al-Khudrī said, "The Messenger of God صَلَّىٰ ٱللَّٰهُ عَلَيْهِ وَسَلَّمَ said, 'God عَزَّ وَجَلَّ causes good deeds to characterize certain people, as well as loving good deeds [themselves], and loving to do them. Similarly, He directs those in need of good deeds towards those who perform them, while making it easy for them to give to those in need, just as He facilitates the falling of the rain on a drought-stricken land in order to revive the land and those who live there.'"[24]

[The Messenger of God] صَلَّىٰ ٱللَّٰهُ عَلَيْهِ وَسَلَّمَ said, "Every good deed is an act of charity, and everything a man spends on himself and his family shall be counted in his favor as an act of charity. So also, everything he spends to preserve his reputation is an act of charity. And whatever a man spends, its results lie with God."[25]

And he صَلَّىٰ ٱللَّٰهُ عَلَيْهِ وَسَلَّمَ said, "Every good deed is an act of charity. Whoever helps others to perform good deeds receives the same reward as he who performs them, and God loves to assist to those in distress."[26]

[The Messenger of God] صَلَّىٰ ٱللَّٰهُ عَلَيْهِ وَسَلَّمَ said, "Every good deed 162
you perform is an act of charity, whether for an affluent person or a poor one."[27]

It is been related that God سُبْحَانَهُ وَتَعَالَىٰ spoke to Moses عَلَيْهِ ٱلسَّلَامُ, saying, "Do not slay the Samaritan, for he is generous."[28]

Jābir said, "The Messenger of God صَلَّىٰ ٱللَّٰهُ عَلَيْهِ وَسَلَّمَ sent out a delegation headed by Qays b. Saʿd b. ʿUbāda. They [the delegation] became

---

23 Narrated by Ibn Abī al-Dunyā in *Kitāb al-Awliyāʾ* [Book of saints] (58) and by al-Bayhaqī in *al-Shuʿab* (10393, 10394).

24 Narrated by Ibn Abī al-Dunyā in *Qaḍāʾ al-Ḥawāʾij* (4); a similar version was included by al-Ḥākim in *al-Mustadrak* (4:321) based on the *ḥadīth* of Caliph ʿAlī رَضِيَ ٱللَّٰهُ عَنْهُ.

25 Narrated by Ibn ʿAdī in *al-Kāmil* (6:431) and by al-Bayhaqī in *al-Shuʿab* (10229). The first sentence of this *ḥadīth* was narrated by al-Bukhārī (6021) and Muslim (1005).

26 Narrated by al-Bayhaqī in *al-Shuʿab* (7251) based on a *ḥadīth* of Ibn ʿAbbās رَضِيَ ٱللَّٰهُ عَنْهُمَا.

27 Narrated by al-Kharāʾiṭī in *Makārim al-Akhlāq* (72), by al-Ṭabarānī in *Makārim al-Akhlāq* (112), and by Abū Nuʿaym in *al-Ḥilya* (3:49) based on a *ḥadīth* of Ibn Masʿūd رَضِيَ ٱللَّٰهُ عَنْهُ.

28 Listed by al-Kharkūshī in *Tahdhīb al-Asrār* (435) and by al-Thaʿlabī in his *Tafsīr* [Commentary] (6:258). Trans.: is A figure spoken of in Q. 20:85ff., "the Samaritan" (*al-sāmirī*) was a hypocrite who led the Children of Israel into idol-worship.

afflicted with barrenness, so Qays slaughtered six riding camels for them. [Upon their return], they told the Messenger of God صَلَّى ٱللَّٰهُ عَلَيْهِ وَسَلَّمَ about this, and he صَلَّى ٱللَّٰهُ عَلَيْهِ وَسَلَّمَ replied, 'Members of that household are known for their openhanded disposition.'"[29]

***

Traditions

ʿAlī رَضِيَ ٱللَّٰهُ عَنْهُ said, "If worldly fortune comes your way, spend thereof, since this [act of spending on good deeds] will not pass away. And if [worldly fortune] is fleeting, spend thereof, for it will not endure." Then he recited these lines:[30]

> Withhold (*tabakhal*) not worldly fortune when it approaches,
> For it will not be diminished by being spent.
>
> 163 Similarly, when it departs, share it freely (*tajūd*),
> For the praise you receive thereby will endure.

Muʿāwiya once asked al-Ḥasan b. ʿAlī رَضِيَ ٱللَّٰهُ عَنْهُمَا about chivalry (*al-murūʾa*), assistance (*al-najda*) and nobility of soul (*al-karam*), and he said, "Chivalry consists in preserving one's religion, being wary of one's self (*nafs*), the hospitable treatment of guests, graciousness during dispute, and stoutheartedness in the face of repugnance. Assistance consists in the defense of one's neighbor, and patience wherever one goes. As for nobility of soul, it consists in doing good for others before they ask, feeding the hungry in times of famine, and showing compassion towards the beggar with the willingness to give freely what one has gained."[31]

> A man once came to al-Ḥasan b. ʿAlī رَضِيَ ٱللَّٰهُ عَنْهُمَا and brought him a parchment.
>
> [Al-Ḥasan] said, "Your need has been met."

29 Narrated by Abū Bakr al-Shāfiʿī in *al-Ghaylāniyāt* (1091) and by Ibn ʿAsākir in *Tārīkh Dimashq* (49:411).

30 The *dīwān* of our Master ʿAlī entitled, *Anwār al-ʿuqūl li-waṣī al-rasūl* [The lights of reason for the trustee of the Apostle] (180).

31 A similar account is narrated by Ibn ʿAsākir in *Tārīkh Dimashq* (13:257), and an identical account is included by al-Kharkūshī in *Tahdhīb al-Asrār* (429).

> Someone then asked him, "O son of the Messenger of God, would it not have been better if you had read the parchment before giving him your answer?"
>
> And al-Ḥasan replied, "God عَزَّوَجَلَّ will ask me about the lowly station in which he appeared before me. So why do I need to read his parchment?"[32]

Ibn al-Sammāk said, "I am perplexed by he who purchases slaves with his money, but who neglects to win over the free with his good deeds."[33]

Some desert Arabs were once asked, "Who is your master?" And 164
they replied, "Whoever endures our cursing, gives to those of us who beg, and indulges the ignorant among us."[34]

ʿAlī b. al-Ḥusayn رَضِيَ اللَّهُ عَنْهُمَا said, "The person who gives of his wealth to those who ask for it cannot be described as generous. Rather, the generous person is one whose first consideration is the claims of God سُبْحَانَهُ وَتَعَالَىٰ over those who seek to obey Him, and who is not selfishly preoccupied with receiving other people's thanks, since he has full confidence in the reward he will receive from God."[35]

> Someone once asked al-Ḥasan al-Baṣrī, "What is generosity?"
>
> And he said, "It is to liberally bestow (*tajūd*) your wealth on others for the sake of God عَزَّوَجَلَّ."
>
> Then someone asked, "And what is prudence (*al-ḥazm*)?"
>
> He replied, "To withhold one's wealth [for the proper reasons]."
>
> He was also asked, "And what is extravagance (*al-isrāf*)?"
>
> And he replied, "Spending out of the desire to gain power over others."[36]

Jaʿfar al-Ṣādiq رَحِمَهُ اللَّهُ said, "There is no wealth that brings a better return than reason, no disaster greater than ignorance, and no act of kindness like imparting advice. Indeed, God عَزَّوَجَلَّ says, 'I am

---

32 Included by al-Kharkūshī in *Tahdhīb al-Asrār* (429).

33 This is how the text was cited by al-Kharkūshī in *Tahdhīb al-Asrār* (430) and by al-Bayhaqi in *al-Shuʿab* (10421).

34 Narrated by Ibn Abī al-Dunyā in *al-Ḥilm* (40) on the authority of Muʿāwiya رَضِيَ اللَّهُ عَنْهُ, who directed this question to Kharīm b. Aws, a desert Arab of Ṭayyiʾ.

35 Cited by al-Kharkūshī in *Tahdhīb al-Asrār* (432).

36 Cited by al-Kharkūshī in *Tahdhīb al-Asrār* (432).

openhanded (*jawād*) and generous (*karīm*), and no mean-spirited soul will enjoy My company. Meanness comes from unbelief, and the people of unbelief belong in the fire. As for openhandedness (*jūd*) and generosity (*karāma*), they come from belief, and the people of belief belong in the garden.'"[37]

165 Ḥudhayfa رضي الله عنه said, "Many a libertine in his *dīn*, who bungles his way through life, will enter the garden due to his magnanimity (*samāḥa*)."[38]

> Al-Aḥnaf b. Qays once saw a man with a dirham in his hand. "Whose dirham is that?" he asked.
>
> "It's mine," the man replied.
>
> Al-Aḥnaf b. Qays then said, "Rather, it will not be yours until it has left your hand."[39]

In this connection, the following line of verse was composed:[40]

> If you cling to wealth, you belong to it.
> But if you spend it, it belongs to you.

Wāṣil b. ʿAṭāʾ was named al-Ghazzāl ("the Spinner") because he used to sit in the company of spinners, and if he saw a woman in need, he would give her something.[41]

Al-Aṣmaʿī said, "Al-Ḥasan b. ʿAlī once wrote to his brother al-Ḥusayn رضي الله عنهما reprimanding him for giving [money] to poets. To this al-Ḥusayn replied, writing, "The best wealth is that which is spent to preserve one's honor."[42]

Sufyān b. ʿUyayna was once asked, "What is generosity?" He replied, "Generosity consists in devotion to brethren, and openhandedness with wealth."[43]

166 He said, "My father inherited 50,000 dirhams, whereupon he sent it out in parcels to his brothers, saying, 'In my prayers, I have

---

37 Cited by al-Kharkūshī in *Tahdhīb al-Asrār* (433).

38 Cited by al-Kharkūshī in *Tahdhīb al-Asrār* (435).

39 Cited by al-Kharkūshī in *Tahdhīb al-Asrār* (435) and by Ibn ʿAsākir in *Tārīkh Dimashq* (24:343), both of whom cited the verse of poetry that follows.

40 See Ibn Qutayba, *Kitāb ʿUyūn al-Akhbār* [The book of choice narratives] (3:181).

41 Cited by al-Kharkūshī in *Tahdhīb al-Asrār* (437).

42 Narrated by Ibn Abī al-Dunyā in *Mudārāt al-Nās* [The virtues of blandishment] (139).

43 Cited by al-Kharkūshī in *Tahdhīb al-Asrār* (438).

asked God سُبْحَانَهُ وَتَعَالَىٰ to grant to my brothers the garden. How could I then withhold from them with regard to [my] wealth?'"[44]

Al-Ḥasan said, "Exerting effort to share what one has is the pinnacle of openhandedness."[45]

> A certain wise man was asked, "Who, of all people, is the most beloved to you?"
>
> He replied, "He who has done great good for me."
>
> It was asked, "And if no one has?"
>
> And he said, "Then he for whom I have done great good."[46]

ʿAbd al-ʿAzīz b. Marwān said, "If someone accepts a good deed I have done for him, he is also doing a good deed for me."[47]

Al-Mahdī once asked Shabīb b. Shayba, "What is your impression of the people in my home?" And he said, "O Commander of the Faithful, I saw people entering hopeful, and exiting content."[48]

ʿAbdallāh b. Jaʿfar conveyed the situation poetically through the 167
following verses:[49]

> A good deed will only be a good deed
> If done in the proper way.
>
> If you do something, intend it for God
> Or kin, lest [your intention] you betray.

ʿAbdallāh b. Jaʿfar said, "These two verses confirm that people are miserly. But, instead, pour out good deeds abundantly. If they benefit the noble, then they will be worthy of [the good deeds],

---

44 Cited by al-Kharkūshī in *Tahdhīb al-Asrār* (438). However, al-Kharkūshī's version reads, "Al-Ḥasan inherited..." instead of "My father inherited..." A similar version is found in al-Ṭarṭūshī's *Sirāj al-Mulūk* (1:373) on the authority of ʿAbd al-Malik b. Baḥr. In MS 'B' we read, "ʿAbd al-Raḥmān b. al-Ḥārith inherited..."

45 Cited by al-Kharkūshī in *Tahdhīb al-Asrār* (440) on the authority of al-Ḥamānī.

46 Cited by al-Kharkūshī in *Tahdhīb al-Asrār* (440). A similar passage is found in al-Dīnawarī's *al-Mujālasa wa Jawāhir al-ʿIlm* [Social intercourse and jewels of knowledge] (84).

47 Cited by al-Kharkūshī in *Tahdhīb al-Asrār* (440).

48 Narrated by al-Khaṭīb in *Tārīkh Baghdād* (9:276).

49 These two verses were composed by our master Ḥassān, and are found in his *dīwān* (1:493).

and if they benefit the ignoble, you yourself will be worthy of [the good deeds]."[50]

***

50 This is how it was cited by al-Kharkūshī in *Tahdhīb al-Asrār* (436), with a similar version having been narrated by Ibn Ḥibbān in *Rawḍat al-ʿUqalāʾ* (254).

7

Tales of the Generous (*al-askhiyā*ʾ) 168

MUḤAMMAD b. al-Munkadir heard the following account from Umm Durra,[1] who was a servant to ʿĀʾisha رضي الله عنها. She said:

> Ibn al-Zubayr sent [ʿĀʾisha رضي الله عنها] money in the amount of 180,000 dirhams in two grain sacks. So she called for a tray and began dividing it among the people.
>
> That evening, she said to me, "O girl, bring my fast-breaking meal."
>
> So I brought her some bread and oil.
>
> I asked her, "Could you not have taken a dinar out of all the money you distributed today and used it to buy us some meat?"
>
> She replied, "If you had reminded me, I would have done that."[2]

The following story was told by Abān b. ʿUthmān, who said:

> A certain man wanted to hurt ʿAbdallāh b. ʿAbbās. So he went to some of the notables of Quraysh and said, "ʿAbdallāh is inviting you to have lunch at his house today."
>
> So they came and filled his house.

---

1 In his *Itḥāf* (8:181), al-Ḥāfiẓ al-Zabīdī gives the pronunciation of this name as Durra, while in *Tabṣīr al-Muntabih bi-Taḥrīr al-Mushtabih* (2:560), al-Ḥāfiẓ b. Ḥajar gives the pronunciation Dharra.

2 Narrated by Hunād in *al-Zuhd* (619), and by Abū Nuʿaym in *al-Ḥilya* (2:47). The same version is also included by al-Kharkūshī in *Tahdhīb al-Asrār* (427).

> "What is this?" inquired ʿAbdallāh, whereupon someone told him about the invitation.
>
> So he ordered fruit to be brought. Then he gave instructions for people to cook. So they cooked, and baked, and the fruit was served to [the guests]. No sooner had they finished the fruit than the tables were set, whereupon they ate and took their leave.
>
> Then ʿAbdallāh asked his people, "Is this kind of fare available in the market whenever I might want it?"
>
> 169 "Yes," they replied. "In that case," he said, "Let them have lunch here every day!"[3]

Muṣʿab b. al-Zubayr said:

> Muʿāwiya رَضِيَ ٱللَّهُ عَنْهُ performed the *ḥajj*, and after departing [Mecca], he passed through Medina. Al-Ḥusayn b. ʿAlī said to his brother, al-Ḥasan رَضِيَ ٱللَّهُ عَنْهُ, "Neither meet him nor greet him."[4]
>
> But when Muʿāwiya left, al-Ḥasan said, "We have a debt, and we must pay it."
>
> So he rode out after [Muʿāwiya], greeted him, and told him about his debt. A two-humped Khorasanian camel bearing 80,000 dinars which belonged to Muʿāwiya's caravan was tired and had fallen behind, and the people driving [the camel] brought it to [Muʿāwiya].
>
> "What is this?" Muʿāwiya asked.
>
> When someone answered him, he said, "Dispatch its load to Abū Muḥammad [that is, al-Ḥasan]."[5]

We have the following account from Wāqid b. Muḥammad al-Wāqidī, who said:

---

3 This is the version of the story included by al-Kharkūshī in *Tahdhīb al-Asrār* (428), and by al-Qushayrī in his *Risāla* (422).

4 Trans.: This was because of the conflict over the caliphate which had arisen between Muʿāwiya and their father, ʿAlī b. Abī Ṭālib.

5 This is how the story reads in al-Kharkūshī's *Tahdhīb al-Asrār* (428). That is to say, Muʿāwiya ordered the camel and its load to be given to al-Ḥasan b. ʿAlī b. Abī Ṭālib so as to enable him to pay his debt.

We were told by my father that he brought a letter to al-Maʾmūn in which he mentioned the heavy debt he owed and his inability to repay it.

In response, al-Maʾmūn wrote on the back of his letter, saying, "You are a man who demonstrates two qualities: generosity and modesty. Generosity is what caused you to open your hand to others. And modesty has prevented you from informing us of the situation you face. I have ordered you to be given 100,000 dirhams. If I am right [in my assessment of the situation], then continue to open your hand to others. And if I am wrong, then you alone will bear the guilt for your transgression. When you were a judge under [Caliph Hārūn] al-Rashīd, you related a *ḥadīth* to me passed down on the authority of Muḥammad b. Isḥāq, on the authority of al-Zuhrī, on the authority of Anas رَضِيَٱللَّهُعَنْهُ, according to which the Prophet صَلَّىٱللَّهُعَلَيْهِوَسَلَّمَ
once said to al-Zubayr b. al-ʿAwwām, 'Zubayr, know that 170
the keys to people's livelihoods are before the Throne. God عَزَّوَجَلَّ sends to each of His servants in accordance with that servant's expenses. To those whose expenses are great, He sends abundance, and to those whose expenses are few, He sends little.' And you know this better than I do."

Then al-Wāqidī added, "I tell you truly, al-Maʾmūn's reminding me of this *ḥadīth* was worth more to me than the award he had granted me of 100,000 dirhams."[6]

A man once asked al-Ḥasan b. ʿAlī رَضِيَٱللَّهُعَنْهُمَا for something he needed, and al-Ḥasan said, "I am keenly aware of your right to ask this of me, and my knowledge of your need weighs upon me. I am unable to provide you with what you deserve. However, that which is a lot [to us] is little in the being of God سُبْحَانَهُوَتَعَالَىٰ. Nothing I possess would be sufficient to show proper thanks [for all you have given

---

6 Narrated in full by al-Khaṭīb in *Tārīkh Baghdād* (3:228) and by al-Kharkūshī in *Tahdhīb al-Asrār* (428). The *ḥadīth* alone was included by Abū Nuʿaym in *al-Ḥilya* (10:216), and a similar version was included by al-Daylamī in *Musnad al-Firdaws* (8554).

me]. So if you will accept what I have and relieve me of the remainder of what I owe you, I will give it to you."

To this the man replied, "O son of the Messenger of God, I accept, and I thank you for your offer. And if you're unable to pay me, I will excuse you."

[Al-Ḥasan] then called for his deputy and had him account for his expenses until he was completely familiar with them. Then he said, "Bring what remains of the 300,000 dirhams."

So he brought [the man] 50,000.

"What did you do with the 500 dinars?" asked al-Ḥasan.

"I have them with me," he replied.

"Bring them here," [al-Ḥasan] instructed him. And he brought them. He then paid both the dinars and the dirhams to the man, saying, "Bring someone who can carry them for you."

So he brought him porters. Al-Ḥasan then gave him his robe to pay the porters.

His servants said to him, "God is our witness, [now] we [as a household] haven't a dirham to our name."

171 And he replied, "But I hope I will have a great reward with God."[7]

The Qurʾān reciters of Basra gathered in the presence of Ibn ʿAbbās, the city's governor, saying, "We have a neighbor who often fasts and spends the night in prayer, and we all wish we could be like him. He has now given one of his daughters in marriage to his brother's son, who is poor and lacks the wherewithal to provide for her dowry."

Upon hearing this, ʿAbdallāh b. ʿAbbās rose, took their hands, and led them into his house. He opened a chest out of which he brought 60,000 dirhams and said, "Carry them away."

So they carried [the money] away.

7 Narrated thus by al-Kharkūshī in *Tahdhīb al-Asrār* (431). A shorter version was included by al-Qushayrī in his *Risāla* (423).

[Afterward] Ibn ʿAbbās said, "We have not been fair to this man. We have given him something that will distract him from his night prayers and fasting. Take us back.[8] Let us simply help him prepare her dowry. For nothing in [this] world should distract a believer from worshiping his Lord سُبْحَانَهُ وَتَعَالَىٰ, nor are we too self-important to serve God's سُبْحَانَهُ وَتَعَالَىٰ saints." So, he did so, and they did so.[9]

It is said that when the people of Egypt were suffering drought and famine under the reign of ʿAbd al-Ḥamīd b. Saʿd, he said, "God is my witness: I hereby declare to Satan that I am his enemy."

He thereupon covered the people's needs until prices went down. He then went into seclusion, and departed owing merchants 1 million dirhams. He gave the merchants his wives' jewelry as a deposit against his debt, their value being 5 million dirhams.[10]

When it became unfeasible for him to recover them, he wrote to the merchants instructing them to sell the jewelry, repay his debt with the proceeds, and give whatever remained thereafter to the needy he had not been able to assist.[11]

Abū Ṭālib b. Kathīr was Shīʿa, and a man once said to him, 172
"By the truth of ʿAlī b. Abī Ṭālib, bring what you are going to give me to such-and-such a place..."

"I shall," Abū Ṭālib replied, "And by his truth, I will give you the same again."

Thus, he gave the man far more than what he had requested.

---

8 Trans.: The implication is that they should recover part of the money Ibn ʿAbbās had sent to the man for fear that an excessive amount would be harmful to his spiritual purity and practice.

9 Included by al-Kharkūshī in *Tahdhīb al-Asrār* (431). See *Thamarāt al-Awrāq* [Fruits of the leaves] (440) and *al-Mustaṭraf* [The exquisite in every appealing art] (1:492-493).

10 In manuscripts other than 'G', the amount is given as 500 million dirhams.

11 Included by al-Kharkūshī in *Tahdhīb al-Asrār* (432).

Abū Murthid was a generous individual in whose praise a certain poet composed some verses.

Abū Murthid said to the poet, "God is my witness, I have nothing to give you. But take me before the judge and claim that I owe you 10,000 dirhams, and I will confess to owing you that amount. Then put me in jail, since I'm sure my family won't leave me behind bars."

So this is what the man did. By that very evening, the man had been paid 10,000 dirhams, and Abū Murthid had been released from jail.[12]

Maʿan b. Zāʾida was a governor over the two ʿIrāqi districts of Basra [that is, Kufa and Basra]. A poet once came to his door and stayed outside his house for a period of time, wanting to go in to see Maʿan. However, he was not allowed entry.

One day the poet said to one of Maʿan's servants, "If the *amīr* goes into the garden, inform me."

So when he went into the garden, the servant informed the poet, whereupon the poet wrote a verse on a piece of wood and cast it into the water that flowed into Maʿan's garden. Maʿan was standing near the water, and when he saw the piece of wood, he removed it from the water and read what was written on it. It said:

> I appeal to Maʿan's openhandedness to tell him of my need
> For apart from that, I have no one to speak for me.

"Who wrote these [lines]?" Maʿan asked.

The man [who had written them] was then summoned.

173 "What was it that you said?" Maʿan asked him. So he recited the lines to him. Then, Maʿan ordered that he be given 10,000 dirhams, and he took them.

Then, the *amīr* took the piece of wood and placed it under his rug. The following day, he took it out from under the rug and read what was written on it. Then he called for the man and paid him 100,000 dirhams. When the man took [the money to him], [the man] second-guessed [the

12 Included by al-Kharkūshī in *Tahdhīb al-Asrār* (432), and by al-Qushayrī in his *Risāla* (423).

> *amīr*'s intentions], and became fearful that [the *amīr*] would take back what he had given him, so he left. On the third day, the *amīr* again read what was written on the piece of wood, and once more called for the man. The man was summoned as before, but he could not be found.
>
> Maʿan said, "It is my duty to go on giving to him until neither a dirham nor a dinar remains in my treasury."[13]

Abū al-Ḥasan al-Madāʾinī said:

> Al-Ḥasan, al-Ḥusayn, and ʿAbdallāh b. Jaʿfar رَضِيَ اللَّهُ عَنْهُمْ went on the *ḥajj*, but they lost their provisions. So they grew hungry and thirsty.
>
> They passed by an elderly woman in a tent and said, "Is there anything [for us] to drink?"
>
> "Yes," she said. So they had their camels kneel, but all she had was a young ewe in the corner of the tent.
>
> "Milk it," she said, "and drink its milk." So they did so.
>
> Then they asked her, "Is there anything to eat?" "No," she said, "except for this ewe. One of you can slaughter it, and I will prepare a meal for you."
>
> So one of them rose, slaughtered the ewe, and cleaned it. Then she prepared food for them, whereupon they ate their fill and stayed until they were rested.
>
> As they were about to set out, they said to her, "We are from the tribe of Quraysh, and this is where we intend to go. If we return safely, pay us a visit, for we wish to return the favor."
>
> Then they departed.
>
> When the woman's husband came home, she told him about the men who had come and about the ewe.
>
> Angered, the man said, "Woe be to you! You slaughter my ewe for people you do not know, then you say, 'They were from the tribe of Quraysh?!'" Some time later, the
> woman and her husband were obliged by need to go into 174
> al-Medīna to take camel dung and sell it there [to make

13 Included by al-Kharkūshī in *Tahdhīb al-Asrār* (432). See *Thamarāt al-Awrāq* (440), and *al-Mustaṭraf fī kulli fannin mustaḍraf* (1:492-493).

their living]. As the woman was walking down one of the city streets, al-Ḥasan b. ʿAlī was sitting at the entrance to his house. He recognized the woman, but she did not recognize him. So he sent his servant boy and invited the woman to come to where he was.

He said to her, "O handmaiden of God. Do you recognize me?"

"No," she replied.

"I was your guest on such-and-such a day," he reminded her.

"O my goodness!" she exclaimed. "Is it you?"

"Yes," he said.

Then al-Ḥasan gave instructions for them to purchase one thousand sheep for her as a gift of charity, and to give her one thousand dinars. He then sent her with his servant to al-Ḥusayn.

Al-Ḥusayn asked her, "How much did my brother give you?"

"One thousand sheep, and one thousand dinars," she replied.

After ordering that she be given the same amount again, al-Ḥusayn sent her with his servant boy to ʿAbdallāh b. Jaʿfar, who asked her, "How much did al-Ḥasan and al-Ḥusayn give you?"

"Two thousand sheep, and two thousand dinars," she replied.

Then ʿAbdallāh b. Jaʿfar ordered that she be given an additional two thousand sheep and two thousand dinars.

He said to her, "If you had begun with me, I would have given you so much, the other two would have found it difficult to match my gift."

So the woman went back to her husband with four thousand sheep, and four thousand dinars."[14]

---

14 Included by al-Kharkūshī in *Tahdhīb al-Asrār* (433). In his *Itḥāf* (8:185), al-Ḥāfiẓ al-Zabīdī stated, "This is the version al-Madāʾinī included with its chains of transmission."

ʿAbdallāh b. ʿĀmir b. Kurayz left the mosque one evening and headed for his house unaccompanied. A young man from the tribe of Thaqīf then came and walked beside him.

"Is there something you need?" ʿAbdallāh asked the young man.

"No," he replied. "All I want is your well-being. I saw you walking by yourself, and I thought I would come and protect you. God forbid that any harm should come to you."

So ʿAbdallāh took him by the hand and walked with him to his house. When they arrived, he called for one thousand dinars to be brought. Then he gave them to the young man, saying, "This is for you to spend, for your family 175
raised you well."[15]

It is said that a group of Arabs came to visit the tomb of a certain generous man. Having travelled a long distance to get there, the visitors spent the night at the man's tomb. One of the visitors dreamed about the man whose tomb they had come to visit, and heard him say, "Can you exchange your *baʿīr*[16] for my *najīb*[17]?"

The generous man who had died had left a *najīb* for which he had been known, while this man owned a fat *baʿīr*.

He replied in his sleep, "Yes," whereupon, in his sleep, he exchanged his *baʿīr* for the man's *najīb*.

After the agreement had been concluded, the man proceeded to slaughter his *baʿīr* in his sleep, after which he woke to find blood streaming out of his *baʿīr*'s neck. He then rose and slaughtered it [in actuality] and divided up its meat, after which they cooked it and ate their fill. They then departed and moved on by night.

The following day as they were on the road, they were received by a party of riders, one of whom said, "Which of you is so-and-so, son of so-and-so?"

15 Included by al-Kharkūshī in *Tahdhīb al-Asrār* (434). In his *Itḥāf* (8:185), al-Ḥāfiẓ al-Zabīdī stated, "This is how al-Ḥasan al-Madāʾinī included it in *Akhbār al-Askhiyāʾ* [Reports on the generous].

16 Trans.: The *baʿīr* is a camel specially suited for riding and bearing loads.

17 Trans.: The *najīb* is a swift, powerful, light-footed camel.

Recognizing his name, the man said, "I am."

Then the rider asked, "Did you exchange anything with so-and-so?"

Then he remembered the man buried in the grave they had visited, and said, "Yes. I exchanged my *baʿīr* for his *najīb* in my sleep."

To this the rider replied, "Take this. This is his *najīb*." Then he added, "He was my father. I saw him in my sleep and heard him say, 'If you are my son, then give my *najīb* to so-and-so,' and named you."[18]

176 As a certain man of the Quraysh tribe was returning from a journey, he passed a desert Arab in the middle of the road whom fate had afflicted with a crippling illness.

The desert Arab said to him, "Whoever you are, assist me against the hand I have been dealt."

The Qurayshite said to his servant boy, "Whatever you have left of our spending money, give it to him."

So the servant boy poured four thousand dirhams into the desert Arab's lap. He attempted to rise, but was too weak to do so. Then he burst into tears.

"What causes you to weep?" the Qurayshite asked him. "Do you consider us to have given you too little?"

"Oh, no!" the man replied, "But I thought about all that people consume of your generosity, and it brought me to tears."[19]

ʿAbdallāh b. ʿĀmir bought a house in the marketplace from Khālid b. ʿUqba b. Abī Muʿīṭ for 90,000 dirhams.

When night fell, he heard Khālid's family weeping.

"What are they crying about?" he asked his family.

They replied, "They are weeping over their home."

ʿAbdallāh then said to his servant boy, "Go tell them that both the house and the money are theirs."[20]

18 Included by al-Kharkūshī in *Tahdhīb al-Asrār* (436).

19 Narrated by Ibn Ḥibbān in *Rawḍat al-ʿUqalāʾ* (248).

20 Narrated by al-Bayhaqī in *al-Shuʿab* (10388).

It has been said that Hārūn al-Rashīd sent Mālik b. Anas رضي الله عنه five hundred dinars. News of this reached al-Layth b. Saʿd, who sent [Mālik b. Anas] one thousand dinars.

[Upon learning of this,] Hārūn became angry and said, "I gave him five hundred, and you give him one thousand when you're my subject?!"

[To this, al-Layth] replied, "O Commander of the Faithful, from my crops I earn one thousand dinars every day. I would have been ashamed to give someone like him less than a single day's earnings."[21]

It has been said that no *zakāt* was due on his income even though it came to one thousand dinars a day.[22]

A woman once asked al-Layth b. Saʿd رحمه الله for some honey, 177
so he issued instructions for her to be given honey in the amount of one *ziqq*.[23]

Someone said to him, "She would have been content with less than that."

[Al-Layth] replied, "She asked in accordance with her ordained needs, and we are giving her in accordance with the ordained bounty that we enjoy."[24]

Al-Layth b. Saʿd had the custom of not speaking on any given day until he had given charity to three-hundred-and-sixty people in need.[25]

Al-Aʿmash said:

A ewe of mine fell ill, and Khaythama b. ʿAbd al-Raḥmān would check on her every morning and evening.

He would ask me, "Has she eaten all of her fodder? How are her young faring without her milk?"

---

21 Included by al-Kharkūshī in *Tahdhīb al-Asrār* (439).

22 Included by al-Kharkūshī in *Tahdhīb al-Asrār* (439).

23 Trans.: The *ziqq* was a unit used to measure honey for purposes of *zakāt*; what it amounts to in terms of modern weights is unknown.

24 Cited by al-Kharkūshī in *Tahdhīb al-Asrār* (439), and by al-Qushayrī in his *Risāla* (423).

25 Cited by al-Kharkūshī in *Tahdhīb al-Asrār* (439).

I had a woollen mat that I used to sit on, and when he left, he would say, "Take whatever is under the mat."

Thanks to his generosity, I received so much to help pay for the ewe's grain—more than 300 dinars—that I hoped she wouldn't recover![26]

ʿAbd al-Malik b. Marwān said to Asmāʾ b. Khārija, "I have heard about certain praiseworthy qualities of yours. Why don't you tell me about them?"

Asmāʾ replied, "It is better for you to hear about them from others than to hear about them from me."

But ʿAbd al-Malik pressed him, saying, "I insist that you speak to me about them."

"O Commander of the Faithful," he said at last, "never have I stretched out my legs [reclining] in the presence of a visitor.[27] Nor have I ever prepared food and invited people to partake of it but that they have been more faithful to me than I have been to them. And whenever anyone has asked me for anything, I have never felt that I gave him more than I should have."[28]

178 Saʿīd b. Khālid once went to see Sulaymān b. ʿAbd al-Malik. Saʿīd was an openhanded man, and if he had nothing to give to someone who had asked for his help, he would write them a promissory note which he would honor at a later time.

And when Sulaymān saw him, he described him in the following line of verse:

> In the morning I heard someone calling out,
> 'Who is there to help the helpful man?'

Then he turned to him and said, "What is it that you need?"

[Saʿīd] said, "I am in debt."

---

26 Cited by al-Kharkūshī in *Tahdhīb al-Asrār* (439).

27 Trans.: In other words, I have always, out of politeness, sat cross-legged, or kept my legs folded beneath me when seated on the floor with a visitor rather than stretching my legs out.

28 Cited by al-Kharkūshī in *Tahdhīb al-Asrār* (440).

"How much is your debt?" asked [Sulaymān].

"Thirty thousand dinars," [Saʿīd] replied.

And [Sulaymān] said, "You shall receive the amount of your debt, and that much again."[29]

It is said that Qays b. Saʿd b. ʿUbāda fell ill, and he found his brothers were taking a long time [to visit him].

He was told, "They are ashamed [to come] because of the debts they owe you."

To this, Qays replied, "God's curses on money that would prevent brothers from visiting each other!"

Then he instructed a herald to announce, "Whoever owes a debt to Qays is hereby released from it."

It is said that his front step broke that evening due to the sheer number [of people] who came to visit him.[30]

Abū Isḥāq said:

I once prayed the dawn prayer in al-Ashʿath's mosque in Kufa, as I was in the city in pursuit of a rival of mine. After I had prayed, a garment and two pairs of sandals were placed before me.

I said, "These things don't belong to me, as I don't pray regularly at this mosque."

But it was said, "Al-Ashʿath b. Qays al-Kindī arrived yesterday from Mecca and gave instructions that whoever prayed in this mosque should receive a garment and two pairs of sandals."[31]

Sheikh Abū Saʿd al-Kharkūshī al-Nīsābūrī رحمه الله said: 179

I heard Muḥammad b. Muḥammad al-Ḥāfiẓ say, "I heard al-Shāfiʿī, who lived next to me in Mecca say: There was a man in Egypt who was known for collecting donations for

29 This is how the account is given by al-Kharkūshī in *Tahdhīb al-Asrār* (440), and *Rabīʿ al-Abrār* [The springtime of the righteous] (1:595-596).

30 Included by al-Kharkūshī in *Tahdhīb al-Asrār* (440).

31 This is how it was cited by al-Kharkūshī in *Tahdhīb al-Asrār* (441). It was also narrated by Ibn Abī al-Dunyā in *al-Ikhwān* [Brothers] (222) without any mention of Abū Isḥāq al-Sabīʿī.

the poor. One time a child was born [to a poor person], who went to this [generous] man and told him a child had been born to him, but that he had nothing to feed the child. So, the man went with him to see a group of potential benefactors, but he came away empty-handed.

Then he came to a certain man's grave and sat there, saying, 'God have mercy on you, you used to do this and that. Today I went from one person to another, and I urged a group of people to give something on behalf of a newborn child, but my efforts were of no avail.'

Then he rose, broke a dinar in half, and handed [the father] one half of it, saying, 'This is a debt you will owe until something better opens up for you.'

So, [the father] took it and left, and did whatever good with it he was able to. That night, this righteous man, whose reward was in the hereafter, dreamt about someone who said, 'I have heard all your pleading, but we do not have permission to give you an answer. Go to my house and tell my children to dig up the spot under the stove. They will find a receptacle containing five hundred dinars. Have them remove it. Then take it to this man [the father].'

The next day, he went to the house of the deceased man [of whom he had dreamt] and told his children the story.

'Have a seat,' they said. As he waited, they dug up the spot he had told them about and retrieved the dinars. Then they brought the money and placed it before him.

'This is your money,' he objected, 'and the vision I saw in my sleep carries no legal weight.'

To this they [the man's children] replied, 'He [our father] is generous even when dead. Shall we not be generous while we're alive?!'

So, at their insistence, he took the dinars to the man with the newborn child, and told him the story. Out of the dinars he had brought, [the father] took one and broke it in half. He gave [the benefactor] the half-dinar he had lent him and took the other one [for himself],

saying, 'This is enough for me. Give the rest away as 180
alms to the poor.'"

Then Abū Saʿd commented, "I don't know which of these people was the more generous."[32]

It has been said that when al-Shāfiʿī رَضِيَ اللَّهُ عَنْهُ was afflicted with the illness that would lead to his death, he said, "Instruct so-and-so to wash me [for burial]."[33]

When he [al-Shāfiʿī] died, news of his death reached this man, so he came and said, "Bring me his financial records."

So they were brought, and it became apparent that al-Shāfiʿī رَحِمَهُ اللَّهُ owed a debt in the amount of 70,000 dirhams. So the man recorded the debt against himself and paid it on [al-Shāfiʿī's] behalf, saying, "This is my washing of him. In other words, this is what he meant [when he gave instructions for me to wash him]."

Abū Saʿd al-Wāʿiẓ al-Kharkūshī رَحِمَهُ اللَّهُ said:

When I went to Egypt, I inquired as to the whereabouts of this man's house, and [people] told me how to get there. I went there for a visit, and met a group of his grandchildren, who exhibited the signs of goodness and virtue. And I said, "His doing of good left its mark on them, and his blessing is manifested in them. As God سُبْحَانَهُ وَتَعَالَى says, *...their father had been righteous* [Q. 18:82]."[34]

Al-Shāfiʿī رَحِمَهُ اللَّهُ said:

I will always love Ḥamād b. Abī Sulaymān for something I once heard about him. It is said that when he was riding his donkey one day, he nudged the donkey and one of his buttons came off. So he passed by a tailor, and was intending to dismount in order for him to repair the button.

32 Narrated by al-Kharkūshī in *Tahdhīb al-Asrār* (441).

33 The person to whom he was referring was Muḥammad b. ʿAbdallāh b. ʿAbd al-Ḥakam. See *Itḥāf* (8:189).

34 *Tahdhīb al-Asrār* (442).

However, the tailor said to him, 'No, no, stay where you are!' Then the tailor came up to him and fixed his button while he was still mounted on his donkey.

Ḥamād then brought out a pouch containing 10 dinars and handed it to the tailor, while apologizing that the amount was so small.[35]

181 Al-Shāfiʿī رَضِيَ اللَّهُ عَنْهُ composed the following verses about himself:[36]

My heart aches over wealth I wish to share
With the destitute among the gallant souls.

An apology to those who seek what I do not have,
Which causes me disasters untold.

Al-Rabīʿ b. Sulaymān said:

When a man came and took hold of al-Shāfiʿī's رَحِمَهُ اللَّهُ stirrup, [al-Shāfiʿī] said, "Rabīʿ, give him four dinars, and apologize to him on my behalf [that I have no more to give him]."[37]

Al-Rabīʿ said:

I heard al-Ḥumaydī say, "Al-Shāfiʿī once brought 10,000 dinars from Sanaʾā to Mecca. He pitched his tent in a spot outside Mecca and spread [the money] on top of a robe. Whenever anyone came to see him, he would grab a handful of coins and give it to them. After praying the noon prayer, he shook out the robe, and none of the money was left."[38]

Abū Thawr once said:

Al-Shāfiʿī, who rarely held onto anything due to his magnanimity, wanted to travel to Mecca and take money with him.

---

35 This is how al-Kharkūshī cited the account in *Tahdhīb al-Asrār* (442); it was also narrated by al-Bayhaqī in *Manāqib al-Shāfiʿī* [al-Shāfiʿī's virtuous acts] (2:232).

36 From the *dīwān* of Imam al-Shāfiʿī (43).

37 Narrated by al-Bayhaqī in *Manāqib al-Shāfiʿī* (2:220).

38 Narrated by al-Bayhaqī in *Manāqib al-Shāfiʿī* (2:220), and by al-Kharkūshī in *Tahdhīb al-Asrār* (443).

I said to him, "With this money, you should buy an estate for you and your children."

So he set out on his journey, and [on his return] when he came to see us, I asked him about this money.

He said, "I found no estate in Mecca that I could purchase
given my knowledge of its origin, as most of the land has
been set aside as a religious endowment. However, I set up
a large tent in the valley of Mina where our companions 182
can stay when they make the *hajj*."[39]

Al-Shāfiʿī رَحِمَهُ ٱللَّهُ once composed these lines:[40]

I find myself craving things
My money cannot buy

Yet I can't bear to withhold from others
What to myself I must deny.

Muḥammad b. ʿImād al-Muhalabī said:

My father went to see [the Caliph] al-Maʾmūn, who gifted him 100,000 dirhams. After leaving the Caliph's presence, he gave the money away as alms. When al-Maʾmūn was informed of this, he reproached my father for what he had done.

But [my father] replied, "O Commander of the Faithful, if I were to withhold what I have, [this would betray] a bad opinion of the One we worship."

So he sent him another 100,000 dirhams.[41]

A man once came to Saʿīd b. al-ʿĀṣ and asked him for alms. Saʿīd ordered that the man be given 100,000 dirhams. And the man wept.

"Why do you weep?" Saʿīd asked him.

---

39 Narrated by al-Bayhaqī in *Manāqib al-Shāfiʿī* (2:223).

40 These lines have been attributed to both al-Shāfiʿī (114) and ʿAbdallāh b. Muʿāwiya (67) of their respective *dīwāns*.

41 This is how al-Kharkūshī cited the account in *Tahdhīb al-Asrār* (444), while a similar account was narrated by al-Khaṭīb in *Tārīkh Baghdād* (3:176).

He replied, "I am weeping for the earth that will swallow up people like you." So he ordered him to be given another 100,000 dirhams.[42]

Abū Tammām went to see Ibrāhīm b. Shakala to recite
verses he had composed in his praise, but when he arrived,
he found him to be ill. [Ibrāhīm b. Shakala] accepted
the verses of praise [the poet had composed], and
instructed his chamberlain to give him the appropriate
183 remuneration, saying, "I hope to recover from my illness
and reward him."

[Abū Tammām] remained there for two months thereafter [without receiving anything], and, weary of waiting, he wrote to [Ibrāhīm b. Shakala], saying:[43]

> It is wrong to accept our praise in verse
> Without the reward to which we aspire
>
> As dinars and dirhams are exchanged for goods
> So does one good turn deserve another.

When Ibrāhīm heard the verses, he asked his chamberlain, "How long has he been waiting at the door?"

"For two months," he replied.

"Give him 30,000 [dirhams]," said [Ibrāhīm]. "Then bring me an inkwell."

He then wrote to [Abū Tammām],[44] saying,

> You hurried us, so your reward was meager
> Else it would have been great
>
> So be content as though you had not spoken
> And we had not been disgraced.

---

42 Included by al-Kharkūshī in *Tahdhīb al-Asrār* (446), and by Ibn ʿAsākir in *Tārīkh Dimashq* (21:132).

43 These verses are not found in Abū Tammām's *dīwān*. See *al-Maḥāsin wa-l-Masāwiʾ* [Merits and faults] (249) and *al-Tamthīl wa-l-Muḥāḍara* (169).

44 These two lines have been attributed to more than one person. They appear in *al-Muṣannaf* by Ibn Wakīʿ (1:108). See the identification of their sources there.

Ṭalḥa is said to have owed ʿUthmān رضي الله عنه 50,000 dirhams. ʿUthmān went out to the mosque one day, and Ṭalḥa said to him, "Your money is ready, so collect it."

In response, [ʿUthmān] said, "It is yours to keep, Abū Muḥammad, to support you in your good character."[45]

Suʿdā bt. ʿAwf said:

I went in one day to see Ṭalḥa, and I noticed that he was weary of spirit.

"What's the matter?" I asked.

He said, "A great deal of money has accumulated in my possession, and it is weighing me down."

"And why should it weigh you down?" I asked.

"Call for your people [to distribute it amongst them]."

So he said to his servant boy, "I must help my people." He then divided the money among them.

Afterwards, I asked the servant, "How much was 184
there?"

"Four hundred thousand," he replied.[46]

A desert Arab approached Ṭalḥa and asked him for help, making a claim on him based on their being relatives.

[Ṭalḥa] said, "No one before you has ever asked me for help based on this tie of kinship. Be that as it may, I have some land which I bought from ʿUthmān for three hundred thousand. If you wish, you can take the land. Or if you wish, I can sell it back to ʿUthmān and pay you its price."

"[I'll take] the price," he said.

So he [Ṭalḥa] sold the land back to ʿUthmān, and paid [the desert Arab] the price [he had received for it].[47]

It is said that ʿAlī رضي الله عنه was weeping one day.

"What causes you to weep?" someone asked him.

45 Narrated by Ibn ʿAsākir in *Tārīkh Dimashq* (25:103).

46 Narrated by Ibn Saʿd in his *Ṭabaqāt* (3:201).

47 Narrated by Abū Bakr al-Shāfiʿī in *al-Ghaylāniyāt* (1083).

And he said, "I haven't received a guest for seven days, and I fear God is showing me disdain."[48]

A man came to see a friend of his and knocked on his door.

"What brings you here?" [the friend] asked.

"I owe four hundred dirhams," [the man] replied.

So his friend weighed out four hundred dirhams and brought them out to him. Then he came back in weeping.

His wife asked, "Why did you give him [that money] if it was going to cause you hardship?"

And he said, "Rather, I'm weeping because I didn't go to check on him, as a result of which he had to broach the matter with me himself."[49]

May God have mercy on those who exhibit these traits, and forgive them one and all.

***

48 Included by al-Qushayrī in his *Risāla* (224).

49 Included by al-Qushayrī in his *Risāla* (421).

8

An Elucidation of the Censure of Miserliness (*al-bukhl*) 185

God سُبْحَانَهُ وَتَعَالَىٰ says, *And whoever is protected from the avarice (shuḥḥ) of his soul - it is those who will be the successful* [Q. 59:9].

He سُبْحَانَهُ وَتَعَالَىٰ says, *And let not those who [greedily] withhold (yabkhalūn) what God has given them of His bounty ever think that it is better for them. Rather, it is worse for them. Their necks will be encircled by what they withheld (bakhilū) on the Day of Resurrection* [Q. 3:180].

Similarly, He سُبْحَانَهُ وَتَعَالَىٰ [will call to account those] *who are miserly (yabkhalūn) and enjoin upon [other] people miserliness (al-bukhl) and conceal what God has given them of His bounty* [Q. 4:37].

The Messenger of God صَلَّى ٱللَّٰهُ عَلَيْهِ وَسَلَّمَ said, "Beware of avarice (*al-shuḥḥ*), for it caused those who came before you to perish, driving them to shed one another's blood and place their sacred charges in harm's way."[1]

He صَلَّى ٱللَّٰهُ عَلَيْهِ وَسَلَّمَ also said, "Beware of avarice, for it lured those who came before you to shed one another's blood, to place their sacred charges in harm's way, and to neglect their kin."[2]

He صَلَّى ٱللَّٰهُ عَلَيْهِ وَسَلَّمَ said, "No miser (*bakhīl*), cheat, traitor, or ill-tempered person will enter the garden."

1 Narrated by al-Bayhaqī in *al-Shuʿab* (10338), and by al-Ṭabarānī in *al-Awsaṭ* (8556).
2 Narrated by al-Kharāʾiṭī in *Masāwiʾ al-Akhlāq* (356).

In another version [he said], "Nor a tyrant," and in another, "nor a benefactor [who gives only to put others in his debt]."[3]

186 He ﷺ said, "There are three things that will cause you to perish: avarice that is obeyed, selfish desires that are followed, and admiration of oneself."[4]

He ﷺ said, "There are three [kinds of people whom] God abhors: the adulterous sheikh, the miser who only gives to others in order to put them in his debt, and the haughty breadwinner."[5]

He ﷺ said, "The person who distributes his wealth and the miser might be likened to two men, each of whom is wearing an iron coat of mail that extends from the chest to the collarbone. When the person who distributes freely spends [his money on others], the coat of mail expands to cover his skin all the way down to his fingertips. As for the miser, whenever he thinks of spending anything, the coat of mail shrinks, its links remaining in place and choking him, and even though he tries to loosen it, he is unable to do so."[6]

He ﷺ said, "There are two traits that cannot be found in a believer: miserliness and ill-temperedness."[7]

He ﷺ said, "Oh God, I seek refuge in You from miserli-
187 ness. I seek refuge in You from cowardice. I seek refuge in You from incapacity in old age."[8]

He ﷺ said, "Beware of committing injustice. For injustice will bring great darkness on the day of resurrection. Beware of obscenity (*al-fuḥsh*), for God does not love the obscene or those given to obscenity. And beware of avarice, for avarice caused those

---

3 This is how it appears in al-Kharāʾiṭī, *Masāwiʾ al-Akhlāq* (361-362); a similar version is found in al-Tirmidhī (1963).

4 Narrated by al-Kharāʾiṭī in *Masāwiʾ al-Akhlāq* (369), by al-Ṭabarānī in *al-Awsaṭ* (5448), by al-Bayhaqī in *al-Shuʿab* (731), and by Abu Nuʿaym in *al-Ḥilya* (2:343).

5 Narrated by al-Kharāʾiṭī in *Masāwiʾ al-Akhlāq* (375).

6 Trans.: In other words, the generous person's coat of mail expands, thereby concealing the person's faults and making it easy to breathe, whereas the miser's coat of mail coils around the neck, gathering at the collarbone, making it difficult to breathe and exposing him or her to danger. Narrated by al-Kharāʾiṭi in *Masāwiʾ al-Akhlāq* (376). Al-Kharāʾiṭī took the *ḥadīth* from al-Bukhārī (1444) and Muslim (1021).

7 Narrated by al-Tirmidhī (1962), and by al-Kharāʾiṭi in *Masāwiʾ al-Akhlāq* (377).

8 Narrated by al-Bukhārī (6365), and by al-Kharāʾiṭi in *Masāwiʾ al-Akhlāq* (381).

who came before you to perish. It commanded them to lie, so they lied; it commanded them to commit injustice, so they committed injustice; it commanded them to cut off ties [with their kin], so they cut off ties."[9]

He صَلَّىٱللَّهُعَلَيْهِوَسَلَّمَ said, "[Two roots of evil] in human beings are: avarice that causes one to cling desperately to what one has [being terrified of losing it], and extreme cowardice."[10]

A man died as a martyr during the days of the Messenger of God صَلَّىٱللَّهُعَلَيْهِوَسَلَّمَ. A woman bemoaned the man's death, saying, "O, what a tragic martyrdom!" The Messenger of God صَلَّىٱللَّهُعَلَيْهِوَسَلَّمَ said, "How can you be certain that he died a martyr? Perhaps he was someone who spoke [publicly] about matters that were of no concern to him, or who withheld from others that which he himself did not need."[11]

> Jubayr b. Muṭʿim once said:
>
> While were on our way back from Ḥunayn with the Messenger of God صَلَّىٱللَّهُعَلَيْهِوَسَلَّمَ, the Messenger صَلَّىٱللَّهُعَلَيْهِوَسَلَّمَ was accosted by some desert Arabs who began begging from him, and they continued to dog him all the way to an acacia tree, where they grabbed his cloak.
>
> At last the Messenger of God صَلَّىٱللَّهُعَلَيْهِوَسَلَّمَ stopped and 188
> said, "Give me my cloak. By the One who holds my soul in His hand, if I had possessions as numerous as these desert shrubs, I would divide them among you, and you would find me neither miserly, nor dishonest, nor cowardly."[12]

> ʿUmar رَضِيَٱللَّهُعَنْهُ said:
>
> The Messenger of God صَلَّىٱللَّهُعَلَيْهِوَسَلَّمَ once made a distribution [of alms], and I said, "Others would have been more worthy of [the alms] than these people are."
>
> And he replied, "They force me to choose between meeting their obscene demands, and being accused of being miserly when I am not."[13]

---

9 Narrated by al-Bayhaqī in *al-Shuʿab* (7055).

10 Narrated by Dāwūd (2511). For a detailed treatment of this passage, see *Itḥāf* (8:194).

11 Narrated by Abū Yaʿlā in his *Musnad* (6646), with a similar account included by al-Tirmidhī (2316).

12 Narrated by al-Bukhārī (2821).

13 Narrated by Muslim (1056).

> Abū Saʿīd al-Khudrī رَضِيَ ٱللَّهُ عَنْهُ said:
>
> Two men went to see the Messenger of God صَلَّى ٱللَّهُ عَلَيْهِ وَسَلَّمَ and asked him for the price of a camel. So he gave them two dinars.
>
> After they left, they encountered ʿUmar b. al-Khaṭṭāb رَضِيَ ٱللَّهُ عَنْهُ, to whom they spoke well of what [the Prophet صَلَّى ٱللَّهُ عَلَيْهِ وَسَلَّمَ] had done for them, expressing their gratitude for what he had given them. [ʿUmar] then went to the Messenger of God صَلَّى ٱللَّهُ عَلَيْهِ وَسَلَّمَ and told him what the two men had said.
>
> He صَلَّى ٱللَّهُ عَلَيْهِ وَسَلَّمَ replied, "I gave so-and-so between ten and one hundred [dinars], and he did not say what these two men said. When people ask me for something, they carry it away under their arm like a blazing ember."[14]
>
> ʿUmar asked, "Why do you give them that which is [tantamount to] fire?"
>
> And he replied, "They insist on asking me for things, and God insists that I not be miserly."[15]

Ibn ʿAbbās said, "The Messenger of God صَلَّى ٱللَّهُ عَلَيْهِ وَسَلَّمَ said, 'Open-
handedness (*al-jūd*) comes from the openhandedness of God
سُبْحَانَهُ وَتَعَالَىٰ. So be openhanded, and God will be openhanded with
189 you. God عَزَّ وَجَلَّ created openhandedness, causing it to appear in the
form of a man and placing its foundation at the base of a blessed
tree. Then He attached its branches to the branches of the Lote tree
of the farthest boundary.[16] He also caused some of its branches to
hang down towards [this] world so if anyone takes hold of one of
them, it will usher him into the garden. Indeed, generosity (*al-sakhāʾ*)
is part of faith, and faith is in the garden. As for miserliness, God
created it out of His wrath, placing its root firmly at the base of the
Zaqqūm tree and causing some of its branches to extend toward

14 Trans.: In other words, their ingratitude for what they have received will bode ill for them on the day of resurrection, when they will suffer the fire of the divine wrath for their failure to be thankful for their blessings.

15 Narrated by Abū Yaʿlā in his *Musnad* (1327), while a similar version was included by Aḥmad in his *Musnad* (3:4).

16 Trans.: This tree marks the utmost boundary in the seventh heaven, and no one can pass it. It is so called because the knowledge of the angels stops at that point and they are not allowed beyond it.

[this world], so that if anyone takes hold of one of its branches, it will lead him away to the fire. Indeed, miserliness is part of unbelief, and unbelief is in the fire.'"[17]

He صَلَّى ٱللَّهُ عَلَيْهِ وَسَلَّمَ said, "Generosity is a tree that grows in the [heavenly] garden, so no one enters the garden but the generous. As for miserliness, it is a tree that grows in the fire, so no one enters the fire but the miserly."[18]

> Abū Hurayra said:
>
> The Messenger of God صَلَّى ٱللَّهُ عَلَيْهِ وَسَلَّمَ asked the delegation from Banū Liḥyān, "Who is your chief, O men of Banū Liḥyān"They replied, "Our chief is Jadd b. Qays. However, he is a man with a miserly streak."
>
> "And what disease is worse than that of miserliness?" he صَلَّى ٱللَّهُ عَلَيْهِ وَسَلَّمَ exclaimed. "Rather, your chief is ʿAmr b. al-Jamūḥ."[19]

> According to another version, they replied, "Our chief is Jadd b. Qays."
>
> To which he replied, "On what basis do you rank him as your chief?"
>
> They said, "He is the wealthiest among us. However,
> we suspect him of miserliness." 190
>
> He صَلَّى ٱللَّهُ عَلَيْهِ وَسَلَّمَ replied, "And what disease is worse than that of miserliness? This is not your chief."
>
> "Who is our chief, then, O Messenger of God?" they said.
>
> And he replied, "Your chief is Bishr b. al-Barāʾ."[20]

---

17 Al-Muttaqī al-Hindī stated in *Kanz al-ʿUmmāl* [Treasures of the doers of good deeds] (16217), "It was narrated by al-Khaṭīb in *Kitāb al-Bukhalāʾ* [The book of misers] on the authority of Ibn ʿAbbās, with a chain of transmission that includes Abū Bakr al-Naqqāsh, who is associated with a number of "denounced" *ḥadīth*s (*manākīr*).

18 This is the wording of the *ḥadīth* as included by al-Daylamī in *Musnad al-Firdaws* (3543).

19 Narrated by al-Bayhaqī *in al-Shuʿab* (10358); al-Bukhārī narrated a similar version in *al-Adab al-Mufrad* (296) based on the *ḥadīth* of Jābir رَضِيَ ٱللَّهُ عَنْهُ.

20 Narrated by al-Ṭabarānī in *al-Kabīr* (2:35), by al-Ḥākim in *al-Mustadrak* (3:219), and by al-Bayhaqī in *al-Shuʿab* (10359).

ʿAlī رَضِيَ ٱللَّهُ عَنْهُ said, "The Messenger of God صَلَّى ٱللَّهُ عَلَيْهِ وَسَلَّمَ said, 'God loathes the person who is a miser throughout his life, but is generous at his death.'"[21]

Abū Hurayra reported that the Messenger of God صَلَّى ٱللَّهُ عَلَيْهِ وَسَلَّمَ had said, "The ignorant person who is generous is more beloved to God سُبْحَانَهُ وَتَعَالَىٰ than the devoted worshipper who is miserly."[22]

Abū Hurayra said, "He صَلَّى ٱللَّهُ عَلَيْهِ وَسَلَّمَ said, 'Avarice and faith cannot coexist in a servant's heart.'"[23]

He also said, "There are two traits which cannot be found in a believer: miserliness and ill-temperedness."[24]

191 He صَلَّى ٱللَّهُ عَلَيْهِ وَسَلَّمَ said, "No believer should be miserly or cowardly."[25]

He صَلَّى ٱللَّهُ عَلَيْهِ وَسَلَّمَ said, "There are those among you who say: The avaricious person is more likely to be excused than the unjust. And [I say:] What injustice is more egregious in God's sight than avarice?! God سُبْحَانَهُ وَتَعَالَىٰ has sworn by His glory, His greatness, and His majesty: 'Neither an avaricious person nor a miser shall enter the [heavenly] garden.'"[26]

> The Messenger of God صَلَّى ٱللَّهُ عَلَيْهِ وَسَلَّمَ is said to have been circumambulating the House of God when he saw a man clinging to the curtains of the Kaʿba and saying, "I beseech you by the sacredness of this house to forgive my sin!"
>
> And he صَلَّى ٱللَّهُ عَلَيْهِ وَسَلَّمَ said, "What is your sin? Describe it to me."

---

21 This is how the *ḥadīth* reads in al-Daylamī's *Musnad al-Firdaws* (627). In *Fayḍ al-Qadīr* [The bounty of the Almighty] (2:285), al-Suyūṭī refers to al-Khaṭīb's version of it in *Kitāb al-Bukhalāʾ*, while the learned al-Munāwī stated, "Al-Daylamī left the place for its chain of transmission blank, as he had not located it."

22 Narrated by al-Tirmidhī (1961).

23 Narrated by al-Nasāʾī (6:13).

24 Narrated by al-Tirmidhī (1962), and by al-Kharāʾiṭī in *Masāwiʾ al-Akhlāq* (377).

25 Narrated by Hunād in *al-Zuhd* (616) on the authority of Jaʿfar al-Bāqir. In his *Itḥāf* (8:197), al-Ḥāfiẓ al-Zabīdī stated, "It was narrated by al-Khaṭīb based on a *ḥadīth* of Abū ʿAbd al-Raḥmān al-Sulamī."

26 Narrated by al-Ṭabarānī in *al-Awsaṭ* (4078) on the authority of Nāfiʿ, who said, "Ibn ʿUmar heard a man say, 'the stingy person is more likely to be excused than the unjust.' To this Ibn ʿUmar replied, 'You lie. I heard the Messenger of God صَلَّى ٱللَّهُ عَلَيْهِ وَسَلَّمَ say, "The stingy person will not enter the garden."'" However, the first part of it is not traceable back to the Prophet.

[The man replied,] "It is too great for me to describe to you."

"Woe to you! Which is greater: your sin, or the [seven] earths?"[27]

"My sin is, O Messenger of God," the man replied.

"Woe to you!" he said, "Which is greater: your sin, or the mountains?"

Again the man said, "My sin, O Messenger of God."

"Which is greater: your sin, or the seas?"

"My sin, O Messenger of God," the man replied.

"Which is greater: your sin, or the heavens?"

"My sin, O Messenger of God," replied the man.

"Which is greater: your sin, or the Throne?" he said.

"My sin, O Messenger of God," he said.

[At last the Prophet asked,] "Which is greater: your sin, or God?"

"God is greater and higher, O Messenger of God," 192
he said.

"Woe be to you! Describe your sin to me," he said.

To this the man replied, "O Messenger of God, I am a man who possesses a fortune, and when others come asking for my help, it's as though they were holding a lighted torch to me."

To this he صَلَّى ٱللَّهُ عَلَيْهِ وَسَلَّمَ replied, "Be gone with you, then. Do not scorch me with your flame. For, by the One who sent me with true guidance and dignity, if you stood between the corner [of the Kaʿba] and the Shrine [of Abraham], prayed for two million years and wept rivers of tears that then watered all the trees [on earth], and then died without reforming yourself, God would cast you headlong into the fire. Woe be to you! Do you not know that miserliness is unbelief, and that unbelief is in the fire? Woe to you! Have you not heard that God سُبْحَانَهُۥ وَتَعَالَىٰ says: *And whoever withholds* [*from others*] *only withholds* [*benefit*] *from himself*

27 The Arabic term *arḍūn* (singular, *arḍ*) rendered here as "earths", refers to the seven earths which are said to exist in parallel with the seven heavens (see Q. 65:12).

> [Q. 47:38], and *whoever is protected from the avarice of his soul - it is those who will be the successful* [Q. 59:9]?"[28]

***

Traditions

> Ibn ʿAbbās رَضِيَ اللَّهُ عَنْهُمَا said:
>
> After creating the garden of Eden, God سُبْحَانَهُ وَتَعَالَى said to her, "Adorn yourself."
>
> So she adorned herself.
>
> Then He said to her, "Manifest your rivers." So she brought forth the Spring of Salsabīl, the Spring of Kāfūr, and the Spring of Tasnīm, out of which there erupted rivers of wine, and rivers of honey and milk.
>
> Then He said to her, "Manifest your couches, your cur-
> 193 tained canopies, your thrones, your jewelry, your garments, and your wide-eyed maidens."
>
> He then looked upon her and said, "Speak."
>
> "Blessed be those who enter me," she replied.
>
> And God سُبْحَانَهُ وَتَعَالَى said, "By My glory and majesty, never will I allow a miser to dwell within you."[29]

Umm al-Banīn, the sister of ʿUmar b. ʿAbd al-ʿAzīz, said, "Fie on the miser! If miserliness were a tunic, I would not wear it, and if it were a road, I would not travel it."[30]

---

28 Narrated by al-Fākihī in *Akhbār Makkah* [Reports from Mecca] (2:278) from a *ḥadīth* of al-Haykal b. Jābir رَضِيَ اللَّهُ عَنْهُ and cited by al-Ḥarīth al-Muḥāsibī in *al-Waṣāyā* (102). As in *Ithāf* (8:197), al-Ḥāfiẓ al-ʿIrāqī stated, "The entire ḥadīth is baseless." See *Asad al-Ghāba* [The lion of the jungle] (5:424) and *al-Iṣāba* (3:581).

29 Narrated by Ibn ʿAsākir in *Tārīkh Dimashq* (52:150) as follows on the authority of Ibn ʿAbbās رَضِيَ اللَّهُ عَنْهُمَا: "When God عَزَّ وَجَلَّ created the Garden of Eden, He placed therein that which no eye has seen, nor has the human heart conceived. Then He said to it, 'Speak.' And it replied, 'The believers have attained success.'" One narrator added the following to the account: "Then it [the heavenly garden] said, 'I am forbidden to every miser and hypocrite.'" A similar version, narrated on the authority of Shuʿayb al-Jubāʾī, is included by al-Kharāʾiṭī in *Masāwiʾ al-Akhlāq* (372).

30 Cited by al-Kharkūshī in *Tahdhīb al-Asrār* (428).

Ṭalḥa b. ʿUbaydallāh رَضِيَ ٱللَّهُ عَنْهُ said, "We find in our wealth that which is found by the miserly, but [unlike them], we are forbearing."[1]

Muḥammad b. al-Munkadir said, "It has been said that if God wills evil for a people, He will cause evil individuals to rule over them, and place their livelihoods in the hands of the miserly among them."[2]

ʿAlī رَضِيَ ٱللَّهُ عَنْهُ once declared in a sermon, "A grievous time will come upon people in which believers will cling to their possessions, though this is not what they have been commanded to do. God سُبْحَانَهُ وَتَعَالَىٰ says, *And do not forget graciousness between you* [Q. 2:237]."[3]

ʿAbdallāh b. ʿAmr said, "Avarice (*al-shuḥḥ*) is worse than miser- 194
liness (*al-bukhl*), for the avaricious person not only clings to what he has, but seeks to deprive others of what they have, whereas the miser simply withholds what he has [from others]."[4]

Al-Shaʿbī said, "I don't know which is deeper in the fires of hell: miserliness, or falsehood!"[5]

> It is said that Anushirvan[6] was once visited by an Indian sage and a Roman philosopher. To the Indian sage he said, "Speak."
>
> And [the Indian sage] said, "The best of people are those who are generous, dignified when angry, unhurried and deliberate in what they say, modest when they enjoy high rank or standing, and kind toward all their kin."
>
> To the Roman philosopher, he said, "Speak."
>
> And he said, "Whoever is miserly, his enemies will inherit his wealth; whoever has little gratitude will not attain success; the people of dishonesty are blameworthy; the people of gossip die in poverty; and whoever has no mercy on others will find himself under the power of one who has no mercy on him."[7]

1 Cited by al-Kharkūshī in *Tahdhīb al-Asrār* (438).
2 Narrated by al-Kharāʾiṭī in *Masāwiʾ al-Akhlāq* (357).
3 Narrated by Abū Dāwūd (3382), and by al-Kharāʾiṭī in *Masāwiʾ al-Akhlāq* (358).
4 Narrated by al-Kharāʾiṭī in *Masāwiʾ al-Akhlāq* (359).
5 Narrated by al-Kharāʾiṭī in *Masāwiʾ al-Akhlāq* (360).
6 Trans.: Anushirvan was the Sasanian monarch of Iran from 531 to 579 CE.
7 Narrated by al-Kharāʾiṭī in *Masāwiʾ al-Akhlāq* (364).

Commenting on the words of [God] سُبْحَانَهُ وَتَعَالَىٰ, *Indeed, We have put shackles on their necks* [Q. 36:8], al-Ḍaḥḥāk said, "Of miserliness: God سُبْحَانَهُ وَتَعَالَىٰ has restrained the hands of [the miserly] from spending in the way of God, for they do not perceive true guidance."[8]

Kaʿb said, "Every morning has been assigned to two angels,
195 who call out, 'O God, for he who clutches [what he has], hasten
destruction, and for he who spends on others, hasten reward.'"[9]

Al-Aṣmaʿī said, "I heard a desert Arab describe a certain man with the words, 'So-and-so has been diminished in my eyes because of the greatness of [this] world in his eyes. For if someone approaches him to ask for charity, [he acts] as though the angel of death had come to him.'"[10]

Abū Ḥanīfa رَحِمَهُ ٱللَّٰهُ said, "I cannot pronounce a miser to be righteous, since miserliness drives him to minute accounting [of what is owed to him], and taking more than what he is entitled to for fear of being cheated. Such people cannot be counted on to take proper care of what has been entrusted to them."[11]

ʿAlī رَضِيَ ٱللَّٰهُ عَنْهُ said, "No generous person (*karīm*) engages in the minute accounting of his due. As God سُبْحَانَهُ وَتَعَالَىٰ declares, *he made known part of it and ignored a part* [Q. 66:3]."[12]

Al-Jāḥiẓ said, "Only three pleasures will remain: Censuring the miserly, eating jerked meat, and scratching scabies-infected skin."

Bishr b. al-Ḥārith said, "[Talking about] the miser is not counted
196 as backbiting (*ghība*)." The Prophet صَلَّى ٱللَّٰهُ عَلَيْهِ وَسَلَّمَ said, "You are most
surely a miser."

Once a woman was praised to the Prophet صَلَّى ٱللَّٰهُ عَلَيْهِ وَسَلَّمَ for being someone who frequently fasted and rose by night to perform ritual

---

8 Narrated by al-Kharāʾiṭī in *Masāwiʾ al-Akhlāq* (370).

9 Narrated by al-Kharāʾiṭī in *Masāwiʾ al-Akhlāq* (384) without the phrase, "and for those who spend [on others], hasten reward (*wa munfiqin, khalafan*)." It was narrated by al-Bukhārī (1442) and Muslim (1010) on the authority of Abū Hurayra رَضِيَ ٱللَّٰهُ عَنْهُ.

10 Narrated in a similar form by Ibn Abī al-Dunyā in *al-Zuhd* (624) on the authority of Abī al-Ḥasan al-Qurashī on the authority of a Helper.

11 A similar version was narrated by the author of *al-Qūt* (2:264), and passed on by Ibn ʿAbd al-Barr in *al-Istidhkār* (27:355).

12 This is how the statement was transmitted in *al-Qūt* (2:264). A shorter version was cited by Ibn ʿAbd al-Barr in *al-Istidhkār* (27:355), while al-Dīnawarī related it as part of a report on the authority of Sufyān (9).

prayer. However, she was also said to be miserly. [Hearing this], he said, "What good is she, then?!"[13]

Bishr also said, "Looking to the miser [as an example] hardens the heart," and, "The ongoing presence of misers is an affliction to the hearts of the believers."[14]

Yaḥyā b. Muʿādh said, "The heart cannot help but love the generous even if they are dissolute (*fajjār*), and it cannot help but hate the miserly even if they are pious (*abrār*)."[15]

Ibn al-Muʿtazz said, "Those who cling to their wealth the most are those who relinquish their honor the most."[16]

> Yaḥyā b. Zakariyā عَلَيْهِمَاالسَّلَامُ met Satan in his true form and said to him, "O Satan, tell me who among people is most beloved to you, and who is most odious to you."
>
> [Satan] replied, "Most beloved to me among people is the miserly believer, and the most odious is the generous sinner."
>
> "Why is that?" [Yaḥyā] asked him.
>
> And [Satan] said, "Because the miser has given me all I seek through his miserliness. As for the generous sinner, I fear that God will look upon him in his generosity and grant him His approval."
>
> Then [Satan] departed, saying, "If you were not Yaḥyā, I would not have told you."[17]

***

13 Narrated by al-Bayhaqī in *al-Shuʿab* (10410).

14 Narrated by Abū Nuʿaym in *al-Ḥilya* (8:350), and by al-Bayhaqī in *al-Shuʿab* (10412).

15 Narrated by Abū Nuʿaym in *al-Ḥilya* (10:66).

16 Cited by al-Thaʿālibī in *al-Tamthīl wa-l-Muḥāḍara* (440).

17 Narrated by Ibn ʿAsākir in *Tārīkh Dimashq* (64:204).

9

197 ## Tales of the Miserly (*al-bukhalā*ʾ)

It is said that there was once a well-to-do, miserly man in Basra. He was invited to a meal by one of his neighbors who prepared him fried meat with eggs. He ate like a glutton.

Then he drank water until his belly was bloated, whereupon he fell ill and was on the verge of death. He began writhing in pain, and when he could no longer bear his suffering, he described his condition to the doctor.

[The doctor] said, "Don't worry! [Simply] vomit up what you ate."

"What?!" the man cried. "Vomit up [this delicacy of] fried meat with eggs? I swear to God, I'd sooner die than vomit up [this dish]!"

It is said that a desert Arab once approached a man who had some figs. [Seeing him approach], the man covered them with his garment. When the desert Arab sat down, the man asked him, "Have you memorized any of the Qurʾān?

"Yes," said the man, and recited the words, "*By the olive and [by] Mount Sinai …*" [Q. 95:1-2].

"And where are the figs?" he asked.

"They're under your garment," [the desert Arab] replied.[1]

1 Trans.: In its complete form, the Qurʾānic passage reads, *By the fig and the olive and Mt. Sinai* [Q. 95:1-2].

A certain man invited a brother to his house, but [all day] fed him nothing into the late afternoon, until [the visitor's] hunger became so intense that it took him to the brink of madness. The host then took a lute and said, "Tell me: What sound would you like me to make for you?"

"The sound of a frying pan," he replied.

It is said that Muḥammad b. Yaḥyā b. Khālid b. Barmak was appallingly miserly.

When asked to describe his dining table, a relative of his
by marriage who knew him well replied, "[His dining table]
spans the space between a person's thumb and forefinger, 198
and the dishes he puts out are the size of a poppy seed."

Then he was asked, "And who comes to [the meals]?"

He replied, "The angels on our right and left who record our good and bad deeds."

"Doesn't anyone eat with him?" he was asked.

"Oh yes," he said, "The flies."

"Shame on him!" [someone exclaimed]. "You're a relative of his, and your garments are tattered!"

"I swear to God," he replied, "I can't even get a needle to mend them with. But if Muḥammad owned a house that extended all the way from Baghdād to Nubia filled with needles, and if he were approached by the angels Gabriel and Michael together with the Prophet Jacob عَلَيْهِ ٱلسَّلَامُ asking him to lend them a needle to mend the robe of the Prophet Joseph that had been torn from behind, he wouldn't do it."

It is said that Marwān b. Abī Ḥafṣa refrained from eating meat out of miserliness unless he had an overpowering craving for it. When he craved it, he sent his servant boy to buy him a [roasted lamb's] head, and ate it.

Someone said to him, "We only see you eating [lamb's] heads in [both] summer and winter. Why is that?"

"Yes, I know how much a head costs," he replied, "so I can be sure the servant boy doesn't cheat me out of any of it by exchanging it for meat he has cooked himself. Nor can he eat any of it [without my knowledge]. If he were to touch an eye, an ear, or a cheek, I would notice. I eat all parts: I eat its eye, its ear, its tongue, its epiglottis, and its brain, and I'm spared the trouble of cooking it myself. So I receive numerous benefits at once [by eating the head]."[2]

One day [Marwān] went out in search of the Caliph al-Mahdī. A woman who was a relative of his asked him, "What will you give me if you return with the prize?"

He said, "If I'm given 100,000 [dirhams], I'll give you one dirham.

199 He was given 60,000 [dirhams], so he gave her 4 *dāniq*s.[3]

[Marwān] once bought a dirham's worth of meat. Then he was invited [for a meal] by a friend of his, so he returned the meat to the butcher for one *dāniq* less, saying, "I hate wastefulness."[4]

Al-Aʿmash had a neighbor who used to invite him to his house, saying, "Come in and have a piece of bread with some salt."

But al-Aʿmash would decline the invitation. However, one day, the neighbor's invitation came at a time when al-Aʿmash was hungry.

"Come by and see us," said [the neighbor]. So, he went to his [neighbor's] house who served him a piece of bread with salt. Just then a beggar came by and requested [alms].

"Bless you," the owner of the house replied.

The beggar then repeated his request.

"Bless you," the owner of the house said again.

When the beggar repeated his request for the third time, the owner of the house said, "Be gone. Otherwise, I swear to God, I'll come out after you with a stick!"

---

2 Narrated by Ibn ʿAsākir in *Tārīkh Dimashq* (57:295).

3 Narrated by Ibn ʿAsākir in *Tārīkh Dimashq* (57:296). Trans.: The *dāniq* (pl. *dawānīq*) was an ancient coin worth one-sixth of a dirham.

4 Narrated by Ibn ʿAsākir in *Tārīkh Dimashq* (57:296).

Then al-Aʿmash called out to [the beggar], saying, "Be gone, woe be to you! For I swear by God, never in my life have I seen anyone truer to his promises. For some time now, he has been promising me bread and salt. And by God, that's all he gave me!"

***

10

200 ## An Elucidation of Altruism (*al-īthār*) and its Virtue

Know that both generosity (*al-sakhāʾ*) and miserliness (*al-bukhl*) are divided into various degrees. The highest degree of generosity is altruism (*al-īthār*), which is openhandedly giving of one's wealth even when one is in need of it. Generosity, by contrast, involves giving what one does not need, whether to someone who needs it, or to someone who does not. Giving away what one needs is more difficult.

Just as a person might be so generous that he ends up bestowing liberally on someone else that which he himself needs, so also with miserliness, [a person] might end up withholding from himself something that he himself needs. Many a miser has fallen ill but held onto his money and not sought out treatment, or felt a desire for something but not satisfied it simply due to being miserly in the face of the price, whereas if it had been available free of change, he would have indulged in it. In this case, [a person] withholds from himself what he needs out of miserliness, while in the other, [a person] prefers someone else (*yuʾthir*) over himself despite his own need. Note the vast difference between these two people. For are not the morals themselves gifts which God سُبْحَانَهُ وَتَعَالَىٰ distributes among us as He wills?

There is no higher degree of generosity than altruism. God سُبْحَانَهُ وَتَعَالَىٰ thus extolled the Companions رَضِيَ ٱللَّهُ عَنْهُمْ for it, saying *they give* [*others*] *preference* (*yuʾthirūn*) *over themselves, even though they are in privation* [Q. 59:9].

The Prophet صَلَّىٱللَّهُعَلَيْهِوَسَلَّمَ once said, "Those who experience an earthly desire but resist it, preferring (*āthara*) [others] over themselves, will be forgiven [for their sins]."[1]

ʿĀʾisha رَضِيَٱللَّهُعَنْهَا said, "The Messenger of God صَلَّىٱللَّهُعَلَيْهِوَسَلَّمَ did not 201
eat his fill for three consecutive days before he departed from [this] world, saying, 'If we had so willed, we could have had our fill. But we preferred [others] over ourselves.'"[2]

Once the Messenger of God صَلَّىٱللَّهُعَلَيْهِوَسَلَّمَ received a guest, but found that his family had nothing [to serve him]. One of the Helpers came and took [the guest] to his own home and placed food before him. [The Helper] then instructed his wife to extinguish the lamp, after which he reached out for the food as though he were partaking of it, when in fact he was not, until the guest had eaten the food. The next morning, the Messenger of God صَلَّىٱللَّهُعَلَيْهِوَسَلَّمَ said to him, "God عَزَّوَجَلَّ marveled at what you did for your guest last night." Then this verse was revealed: *They give* [*others*] *preference* (*yuʾthirūn*) *over themselves, even though they are in privation* [Q. 59:9].[3]

Generosity is a characteristic from among the characteristics of
God سُبْحَانَهُۥوَتَعَالَىٰ,[4] and altruism is the highest degree of generosity. It 202
was also a consistent trait of the Messenger of God صَلَّىٱللَّهُعَلَيْهِوَسَلَّمَ so that God سُبْحَانَهُۥوَتَعَالَىٰ called him 'great', saying سُبْحَانَهُۥوَتَعَالَىٰ to him, *And indeed, you are of a great moral character* [Q. 68:4].[5]

---

1 Narrated by Ibn ʿAdī in *al-Kāmil* (5:127). It was also cited by al-Kharkūshī in *Tahdhīb al-Asrār* (447) as part of the story of Ibn ʿUmar رَضِيَٱللَّهُعَنْهُ when he craved fish, and by Ibn ʿAsākir in *Tārīkh Dimashq* (31:142) in the same context as that cited by al-Ghazālī.

2 This is how the account was cited by al-Kharkūshī in *Tahdhīb al-Asrār* (449); it was also cited by al-Bukhārī (5374) and Muslim (5416) from her رَضِيَٱللَّهُعَنْهَا *ḥadīth* that reads, "After coming to Medina, the family of Muḥammad صَلَّىٱللَّهُعَلَيْهِوَسَلَّمَ did not eat their fill of bread for three consecutive nights before he was taken." Al-Bayhaqī cited the account in *al-Shuʿab* (1396) with a chain of transmission that includes Bishr on her رَضِيَٱللَّهُعَنْهَا authority, and which reads: "Had we so willed, we could have eaten our fill. But Muḥammad صَلَّىٱللَّهُعَلَيْهِوَسَلَّمَ preferred [others] over himself…" And some of it was cited previously.

3 This is how the account was cited by al-Kharkūshī in *Tahdhīb al-Asrār* (449); and by al-Bukhārī (3798) and Muslim (2054).

4 In *Tārīkh Iṣbahān* (1:178), Abū Nuʿaym related a prophetic *ḥadīth* of ʿAmmār b. Yāsir رَضِيَٱللَّهُعَنْهُ that reads, "Generosity is God's greatest moral attribute."

5 This is how the account was cited by al-Kharkūshī in *Tahdhīb al-Asrār* (452) transmitted from al-Junayd.

Sahl b. ʿAbdallāh al-Tustarī said,

> Moses عَلَيْهِ ٱلسَّلَامُ once said, "O Lord, show me some of the degrees (*darajāt*) of Muḥammad صَلَّى ٱللَّهُ عَلَيْهِ وَسَلَّمَ and his community [of Muslims]."
>
> [God] replied, "O Moses, you would not be able to bear it. However, I will show you a spiritual station (*manzila*) from among his great and majestic stations, on the basis of which I have made his virtue superior to you and all people on earth."
>
> He then showed him [Moses] the Kingdom of Heaven (*malakūt al-samāʾ*), where he beheld a spiritual station so glorious that it nearly annihilated his soul with the brilliance of its lights and its nearness to God عَزَّوَجَلَّ.
>
> [Moses asked], "O Lord, On what basis did you cause him to ascend to this [rank of] spiritual dignity?"
>
> He replied, "I did so on the basis of a trait that I bestowed specially upon him among all people, namely, altruism. O Moses, if anyone approaches Me after having practiced this virtue for any period of time, I will be ashamed to hold him accountable [for his other deeds on earth]. Indeed, I will grant him a seat of his choice in my garden."[6]

ʿAbdallāh b. Jaʿfar went out to a rural estate of his and entered a palm grove belonging to some people, where he saw a black slave boy who was working there. The boy brought his daily rations, [which consisted of three small loaves of bread]. A dog then entered the grove and approached the boy. The boy threw the dog one of the loaves, which it ate. While ʿAbdallāh looked on, the boy threw it the second, followed by the third, and the dog ate these as well.

"How much is your daily ration, boy?" he asked.

"What you just saw," he replied.

"So why did you prefer [to give] it to this dog [rather than eat it yourself]?" [ʿAbdallah] asked.

[The boy] replied, "It came from somewhere far away, and it arrived hungry, and I hated to turn it away."

6 Cited by al-Kharkūshī in *Tahdhīb al-Asrār* (454).

> "So what will you do today?" [ʿAbdallāh] inquired.
>
> "I'll spend my day [hungry]," said [the boy].
>
> ʿAbdallāh b. Jaʿfar said, "[And to think that] I am blamed
> for being [too] generous! Truly this [boy] is more generous 203
> than I am!" So he purchased the grove, the slave boy, and the tools on the land. Then he freed the boy and gave him a share [of the land and the tools].[7]

ʿUmar رَضِيَ ٱللَّهُ عَنْهُ said, "One of the Companions of the Messenger of God صَلَّى ٱللَّهُ عَلَيْهِ وَسَلَّمَ was given a sheep's head, and he said, 'Brother so-and-so needs it more than I do,' so he sent it to him. Thereafter, the sheep's head continued to be sent from one person to another until it had made the rounds of seven households, and at last it returned to the first one."[8]

> ʿAlī b. Abī Ṭālib رَضِيَ ٱللَّهُ عَنْهُ once slept in the Prophet's bed صَلَّى ٱللَّهُ عَلَيْهِ وَسَلَّمَ.[9] So God سُبْحَانَهُ وَتَعَالَىٰ spoke to the angels Gabriel and Michael عَلَيْهِمَا ٱلسَّلَامُ, saying, "I have caused the two of you to be brothers. As such, I have given one of you a longer life than the other. So which of you will prefer his brother over himself?"
>
> However, both of them chose to be given the longer life.
>
> God عَزَّ وَجَلَّ then spoke to them again, saying, "Won't the two of you be like ʿAlī b. Abī Ṭālib? I placed a spirit of brotherhood between him and my Prophet, Muḥammad صَلَّى ٱللَّهُ عَلَيْهِ وَسَلَّمَ, and so he slept in the Prophet's bed, thereby risking his life for his sake and preferring to grant him life [rather than preserve his own]. So go down to earth and protect [ʿAlī] from his enemy."
>
> So Gabriel عَلَيْهِ ٱلسَّلَامُ stood guard at his head, while Michael stood guard at his feet. As they stood there, Gabriel exclaimed, "Who could compare with you, son of Abī Ṭālib—the one of whom God boasts to the angels?!"

---

7 *Al-Risāla al-Qushayriya* [The treatise of al-Qushayrī] (421).

8 Narrated by al-Ḥākim in *al-Mustadrak* (2:184) on the authority of Ibn ʿUmar رَضِيَ ٱللَّهُ عَنْهُمَا, and by al-Bayhaqī in *al-Shuʿab* (3204).

9 Trans.: He did this in order to protect the Prophet صَلَّى ٱللَّهُ عَلَيْهِ وَسَلَّمَ from certain persons who had been planning to kill him صَلَّى ٱللَّهُ عَلَيْهِ وَسَلَّمَ in his sleep.

> It was then that God سُبْحَانَهُ وَتَعَالَىٰ revealed the verse that reads, *And of the people is he who sells himself, seeking means to the approval of God. And God is kind to* [*His*] *servants* [Q. 2:207].[10]

204 Abū al-Ḥasan al-Anṭākī reported that thirty-some people once gathered at his house. They were in a village near al-Rayy,[11] and they had just a few loaves of bread that wouldn't be enough to satisfy them all. So they broke up the loaves of bread, extinguished the lamp, and sat down for the meal. When the gathering broke up, however, the food remained untouched. None of them had eaten a thing, [each one] preferring his companions over himself.[12]

It is said that Shuʿba was once approached by a beggar at a time when he had nothing himself. So he removed a plank of wood from the roof of his house and gave it to the beggar, apologizing to him [that he could not do more].[13]

Ḥudhayfa al-ʿAdawī said:

> On the day when the Battle of Yarmūk took place, I set out in search of a paternal cousin of mine and I had a bit of water with me. I said to myself: If he is still alive, I will give him water to drink and wipe his face with it.
>
> When I found him, I said, "Shall I give you a drink?" He nodded in the affirmative. Then a man nearby let out a soft moan, whereupon my cousin gestured for me to take the water to him, saying, "Take it to him."
>
> So I went over to him, and found that it was Hishām b. al-ʿĀṣ.
>
> "Shall I give you a drink?" I asked.
>
> Just then [Hishām] heard another man let out a moan, and Hishām gestured for me to take the water to him. So I went over to [the man], but he had died. I then went back to Hishām, but he had died. After this I went back to my

10 This is how the account reads in al-Kharkūshi's *Tahdhīb al-Asrār* (450) and al-Thaʿlabī's *Tafsīr* (2:125).

11 Trans.: A city in Khorasan.

12 Cited by al-Kharkūshī in *Tahdhīb al-Asrār* (448).

13 Cited by al-Kharkūshī in *Tahdhīb al-Asrār* (448).

cousin, but he had died. May God have mercy on them all رَحِمَهُمُ ٱللَّهُ.[14]

ʿAbbās b. Dahqān said, "No one has ever left [this] world [as pure]
as he entered it with the exception of Bishr b. al-Ḥārith. Once a 205
man, when he was ill, came to [Bishr] and complained to him of
his need. So [Bishr] took off his shirt and gave it to the man, after
which he borrowed a robe and died in it."[15]

A certain Sufi said, "We were in Tarsus, where we met as a group and went out to Bāb al-Jihād (the Jihād Gate). A dog followed us out of the city, and when we reached Bāb al-Jihād, we came upon a dead pack animal. We went over to an empty spot and sat down. When the dog saw the dead animal, it went back to the city. It returned an hour later and with it were twenty more dogs. Then it retired to one side while the other dogs tore into the dead animal. As the lone dog looked on, the others continued eating until nothing remained of the dead animal but the bones. When the other dogs returned to the town, the lone dog rose, went over to the bones and finished off what clung to them. Then it went on its way."[16]

We have cited a number of accounts of altruism and the events [in the lives] of the saints in *The Book on Poverty and Abstinence*, so there is no need to repeat them here. All success comes through God, and in all endeavors that earn His good pleasure, one's reliance is on Him عَزَّوَجَلَّ.

***

14 This is the version cited by al-Kharkūshī in *Tahdhīb al-Asrār* (448). It was likewise narrated by Ibn al-Mubārak in *al-Zuhd* (525) and by al-Bayhaqī in *al-Shuʿab* (3208).

15 Cited by al-Kharkūshī in *Tahdhīb al-Asrār* (451) with the name ʿAyyāsh in place of ʿAbbās, which is consistent with MS 'b'.

16 Cited by al-Kharkūshī in *Tahdhīb al-Asrār* (454).

11

206 ## An Elucidation of the Definition of Generosity (*al-sakhāʾ*) and of Miserliness (*al-bukhl*) and the True Nature of Each

YOU may say, We know based on evidence from the divine law that miserliness is one of the perils (*mahlakāt*) [that to lead to perdition]. But what is the defining feature of miserliness? And what is it that makes a person miserly?

Every human being sees himself as being generous, yet others may see him as miserly. Similarly, someone may do something about which people have differing opinions. Some people might say that a given action was miserly, while others may say that it was not. Conversely, every person has some love for wealth, as a result of which he seeks to protect it and hold onto it. If holding onto wealth makes a person miserly, then no one can escape miserliness. If holding onto wealth does not necessarily entail miserliness—though miserliness has no meaning without the holding onto wealth—then what is the miserliness that leads to perdition?

Conversely, what is the defining feature of generosity, on the basis of which someone can rightly be described as generous and merit [generosity's] reward?

In answer, we say: Some have claimed that the defining feature of miserliness is that which relates to a duty [that is, withholding what one has a duty to relinquish]. [If this is the case,] then no one who gives others what he is obliged by duty to give them can be classified as miserly. However, this is not sufficient. For example, the person who returns meat to the butcher or bread to the baker with a morsel or crumb missing would, by everyone's agreement, be described as miserly. Similarly, someone who provides his family with the amount required by law, then harasses them over every extra bite they take, or every bit they consume of his money, will be viewed as miserly. And, whoever has a loaf of bread and, when someone comes along whom he thinks would want to eat it, hides it from view—[this person] is also a miser.

It has been said that the miser is one who finds it difficult to give. 207
However, this [definition] also falls short. For if what is meant by this is that he finds every act of giving to be difficult, then [it can be pointed out that] even a miser may find it easy to give small amounts. Such a person might gladly give away a morsel or so, but find it difficult to give up more than this. If, by contrast, what is meant is that the miser is someone who finds *some* giving to be difficult, it should be remembered that even the openhanded person may find some things difficult to give: [it might be difficult, for example,] to make a gift that consumes all of his or her money, or a great proportion of it. Therefore, this is also insufficient to determine miserliness.

Similarly, there have been discussions of what openhandedness entails. It has been said that openhandedness is giving without expecting anything in return, and coming to others' aid without hesitation.

It has been said that openhandedness is giving without asking how [giving] will diminish [what one has].

It has been said that openhandedness is taking pleasure in being asked for help, and rejoicing in giving whatever one can.

It has been said that openhandedness is giving based on seeing that all wealth belongs to God سُبْحَانَهُ وَتَعَالَىٰ, that the servant himself belongs to God سُبْحَانَهُ وَتَعَالَىٰ, and so the servant of God gives away the wealth of God without any thought of poverty.

It has been said that he who gives a part of what he has, while keeping a part thereof, is a person of generosity; he who gives most of what he has and keeps something for himself is a person of openhandedness; and he who suffers harm for the sake of giving preference to others is a person of altruism. And he who gives nothing, he is a person of miserliness.

***

What has been said thus far still fails to encompass the essential features of miserliness and openhandedness. Rather, what we
208 propose is that wealth was created for a wise reason and purpose, and that is to meet people's needs. As such, one might refrain from spending it [on one thing] in order to spend it on that for which it was intended. Conversely, one might give it freely by spending it on something it is not good to spend it on. One might dispose of it in a just manner, which involves withholding it in situations in which it ought to be withheld, and giving it freely in situations in which it ought to be given freely. Withholding money in situations in which it ought to be given freely is miserliness, while giving it in situations in which it ought to be withheld is squandering (*tabdhīr*). Between these two [extremes of miserliness and wastefulness] is a mean that is praiseworthy, and generosity and openhandedness are its expression. The Prophet صَلَّى ٱللَّٰهُ عَلَيْهِ وَسَلَّمَ was ordered [by God] to practice [the mean of] generosity, for he was told: *And do not make your hand* [*as*] *chained to your neck or extend it completely* [Q. 17:29]. Similarly, God سُبْحَانَهُ وَتَعَالَىٰ declares, *And* [*they are*] *those who, when they spend, do so not excessively or sparingly but are ever, between that,* [*justly*] *moderate* [Q. 25:67].

Openhandedness, then, is a middle point between extravagance (*al-isrāf*) and stinginess (*al-iqtār*), between expansion (*al-bast*) and constriction (*al-qabd*). It involves a proper appraisal of what one gives and what one withholds in light of what duty requires. However, it is not enough for someone to engage in the outward act of giving without his heart being in harmony with this action, free of any other intention. If he gives his money in the ways it ought to be given, but the ego struggles with it and has to exert effort to bear it, then he is attempting to be generous, but he is not [truly] generous. Rather, his heart should have no attachment to wealth, except insofar as [it is attached to] the wealth serving its intended purpose, which is to be spent on what it ought to be spent on.

***

If you say: this all depends on knowledge of what the obligation (*al-wājib*) is. Then the question is: what [is the amount that] must be given?

And to this I would reply: obligation consists of two types. The first type is based on law, while the second type is based on social graces and social custom. The generous person is one who neglects neither the obligation of the law nor the obligation of social
graces. For if he neglects either of the two, he is a miser. However, 209
whoever fails [to give] what is required by law is more miserly, such as someone who fails to distribute *zakāt,* and someone who deprives his wife and children of the material support they need, or someone who does these things, but grudgingly, since, being miserly by nature, he feigns generosity. Then there are those who give away their defective possessions, but resist giving up their highest-quality possessions, or even their moderately nice ones. All of this is miserliness.

As for the obligation dictated by social graces, it involves refraining from showing irritation or harshness, or nitpicking over trivial matters, since such behavior is shameful. However, the shamefulness of such behavior varies depending on the persons concerned, their circumstances, and their stations in life. So, for example, the irritation that might be an acceptable reaction on the part of a poor person, would be shameful coming from a wealthy individual, while the irritation a man might show toward a stranger would not be considered as shameful as it would if he showed it toward his close family, his relatives, or his slaves. Behaving irritably toward a neighbor would be deemed more shameful than it would toward someone distant, while showing irritation while offering hospitality would be deemed more shameful than while buying, selling, and engaging in other formal or business transactions. Similarly, it is deemed more shameful to show irritation when providing food or clothing than when providing other things. When purchasing funeral shrouds, for example, an animal for sacrifice (*uḍḥiya*), or bread to give as alms, it is deemed more shameful to show irritation than it is when purchasing other things. Similarly, the unacceptability of such a response varies depending on who it is that one shows irritation toward: that is, depending on whether it is a friend, a brother, a relative, a spouse, one's child, or a stranger. It also varies depending on who expresses the irritation: that is, whether it is expressed by a child, a woman, an elderly person, a young person, an educated person, an uneducated person, a wealthy person, or a poor person.

Thus, the miser is the person who neglects [to give] when he
210 should not neglect [to give], either based on law, or based on the dictates of chivalry and social graces, the latter of which cannot be quantified.

Perhaps the defining feature of miserliness is that it involves holding onto [your] wealth [rather than contributing it to] some purpose—that purpose being more important than saving money. Preservation of the religion, for example, is more important than saving money. Hence, someone who refuses to distribute *zakāt* or support his family is a miser. Similarly, maintaining social graces is more important than saving money; hence, someone who quibbles irritably over trivial details [of wealth] with people towards whom it is not good to show irritation, thus violating the rules of social graces due to the love of money, is a miser.

There remains another level: and that is he who fulfills his religious obligations and maintains social graces, but who has amassed great wealth which he does not spend on charity and other assistance to the needy. The aim of saving money in order to safeguard [a person] from the vicissitudes of fate, conflicts here with the aim of seeking a reward and elevating his station in the hereafter. For holding onto wealth in the service of this aim [of safeguarding against the vicissitudes of fate] is a form of miserliness in the view of the sagacious, though not in the view of the general populace. That is because their sights tend to be set exclusively on the fortunes of [this] world, and therefore view it as important to refrain from spending money to protect themselves from the vicissitudes of fate. However, someone's miserliness might become apparent to the general populace if there were a person in need nearby to whom he said, "I have paid the *zakāt* I owe, and I owe nothing beyond it." The shamefulness of such behavior will depend on how wealthy he is, as well as on how severe [the other individual's] need is, as well as his righteousness, his *dīn*, and his worthiness of assistance. Generally speaking, those who have fulfilled their duty by the standards of law, as well as the requirements of chivalry and social graces in keeping with their social status, may be deemed innocent of the charge of miserliness.

Yes, [a person] cannot be described with the qualities of openhandedness and generosity unless he gives more than this in pursuit of virtue and an elevated spiritual station. But if his soul is so expansive that he willingly gives of his wealth beyond what is required by law, not doing so in order to avoid condemnation by 211
the general populace, then he will be openhanded to the degree to which his soul expands, be it lesser or greater. There are limitless degrees of such variation, with some people being more openhanded than others.

Openhandedness is scrupulousness in doing good beyond what is dictated by social graces. But, it must be done willingly and gladly, not out of greed (*ṭamʿ*) or in the hope of receiving some service, reward, thanks, or commendation. For whoever is greedy for thanks and commendation is a merchant, not an openhanded soul, since they are essentially purchasing praise with their wealth. Praise is a luxury which is pursued for its own sake, whereas openhandedness is giving something freely without hope of compensation. This is the true [meaning of openhandedness] and it could not conceivably occur except by coming from God سُبْحَانَهُ وَتَعَالَىٰ.

It should be remembered, of course, that when applied to human beings, the term openhandedness (*jawād*) is being applied metaphorically. After all, when [a person] gives something, he always does so for a purpose. If his sole purpose is to earn reward in the hereafter, or to acquire the virtue of openhandedness and to purify his soul from the vice of miserliness, then he may be called openhanded. But if he is motivated by a fear of ridicule, for example, or [fear] of condemnation by other people, or by the hope of some benefit he expects to receive from the person he is helping—then none of is considered openhandedness. For [in these cases] he is led by these motivations, all of which are various forms of immediate compensation for what he has done. In cases such as these, then, we are not openhanded, but simply in search of compensation.

In this vein, it is said:

> A certain pious hermit came to speak with Ḥibbān b. Hilāl as he was sitting with his companions.

She said, "Is there someone here of whom I might ask a question?"

"Ask whatever you would like," they said to her, pointing to Ḥibbān b. Hilāl.

Then she asked, "What is generosity in your opinion?"

212 They replied, "It is giving, distributing freely, and altruism."

She replied, "This is generosity in worldly terms. But what is it in spiritual terms?"

They said, "It is to worship God سُبْحَانَهُ وَتَعَالَىٰ with giving souls, not out of obligation."

"So, do you want a reward for this?" the woman asked.

"Yes," they said.

"Why is that?" she asked.

They replied, "Because for every good deed we perform, God سُبْحَانَهُ وَتَعَالَىٰ has promised ten times the like thereof."

"Glory be to God!" she said. "If you've given one thing and received ten in return, what generosity have you shown toward Him?!"

Then they asked her, "So what is generosity in your view, God have mercy on you?"

"As I see it," she replied, "generosity is to worship God سُبْحَانَهُ وَتَعَالَىٰ basking in grace, enjoying the pleasure of obeying him, without the slightest reluctance, without desiring any reward, so that your Master can do with you whatever He wills. Aren't you ashamed to have God look into your hearts and see that you want one thing in return for another?! In [this] world, that would be repugnant."

Another pious woman said, "Do you suppose that generosity has to do with nothing but dinars and dirhams?"

In reply, someone asked, "What *does* it have to do with, then?"

And she said, "As I understand it, generosity has to do with one's innermost being (*al-muhaj*)."

Al-Muḥāsibī said, "In the *dīn*, generosity means for your soul to give freely of itself to God عَزَّوَجَلَّ, even to the point of annihilation, and for your heart to spend its innermost being (*muhaja*) and spill its blood for God's sake سُبْحَانَهُوَتَعَالَىٰ with utter magnanimity, without any reluctance, and without desiring any reward, temporal or everlasting. However, if you cannot do without a reward, but your heart is ruled by the desire to be excellently and perfectly generous, leave the choice to God سُبْحَانَهُوَتَعَالَىٰ, such that He is truly your Lord, who chooses for you what you are not able to choose well for yourself."

***

12

213 ## An Elucidation of the Remedy for Miserliness

KNOW that the cause of miserliness is the love of wealth. The love of wealth has two causes:

The first of them is love for the pleasures that can only be attained with money, combined with long-term hope. If someone knew that he would die tomorrow, he might not cling to his money. The amount of money he would need for a day, a month, or a year relates to the near-term future. However, he may have children, who represent long-term hope, since he counts their survival as part of his own, and he wants to save [money] for their sake. That is why the Messenger of God صَلَّى ٱللَّٰهُ عَلَيْهِ وَسَلَّمَ said, "Children are a cause of miserliness, cowardice, and ignorance."[1] Add to that the fear of poverty and lack of confidence that his daily sustenance will be provided, then he is bound to become all the more miserly.

The second cause is the love of money for its own sake. There are people who have more than enough to last them for the rest of their lifetimes, if they continue living in the same way they have been accustomed to. [A person] might be an elderly individual with no children and a great deal of money. Yet he might still be unable to bring himself to distribute *zakāt*, or get medical treatment if he falls ill. Instead, he has come to love money with such a passion that he takes pleasure in the mere fact of having it in his possession, as well

---

1 Narrated by Ibn Mājah (3666), whose version lacks the word *majhala* ("a cause of ignorance"). The same *ḥadīth* is cited by ʿAbd al-Razzāq in *al-Muṣannaf* (11:140), by al-Ṭabarānī in *al-Kabīr* (24:241), and by al-Ḥākim in *al-Mustadrak* (3:296).

as the power he has over it. So, he hides it in the ground, knowing full well that he will die, and that it will be either lost or taken by 214
his enemies. Yet nevertheless, he cannot bring himself to spend the least bit of it either on himself, or on others in the form of charity.

This is a dreadful disease of the heart which is difficult to treat, especially as one grows older. Indeed, it becomes a chronic illness for which no remedy can be hoped. The situation might be likened to that of a man who has fallen in love with someone, but who then falls in love with this person's messenger. He then becomes so preoccupied with the messenger that he forgets all about the person he loves. Money is a messenger that gives [a person] access to the things he needs, as a result of which it becomes beloved to him, since whatever gives him access to what is pleasant, is itself pleasant. Then he ends up forgetting the things he needs and treating the gold that he has as worthy of being loved for its own sake. However, this is the ultimate delusion. Whoever thinks there is a difference between money and a [mere] stone are simply ignorant. Money's only value lies in its ability to meet [a person's] needs, and any sum that he possesses beyond the amount [required] for what he needs is exactly equivalent to a stone.

***

These are the causes underlying the love of wealth, and the remedy for each malady lies in activating an opposing factor. Thus, the love of worldly pleasures is treated through patience and satisfaction with little, while hope in the long-term future can be addressed by bringing death frequently to mind: to look at the death of people similar to us who labored for years to accumulate wealth only for it to be lost after they died. As for the tendency to cling to one's children and fret over their care and well-being, it can be overcome by contemplating the fact that the One who created one's children created their sustenance along with them, and by thinking of all the children who did not inherit anything from their parents, but who are better off than those who did. Whoever accumulates wealth for his child with the intention of leaving him in a good condition, [know that] this good intention might yield the opposite outcome. For if his child is righteous and God-fearing, God's provision will suffice him, but if he is corrupt, he will use his money to assist in disobedience, and his wrongdoing will fall back onto [the parent].

215 His heart can also be treated by frequent contemplation of the accounts that have been passed down censuring miserliness, praising generosity, and warning of the terrible punishment for miserliness that God has promised.

Another effective antidote [for the heart] is frequent reflection on the conditions of the miserly and the natural tendency to dislike or be offended by them. For even misers hate miserliness in others, and find their miserly friends insufferable. As a result, misers will end up realizing that people secretly view them as filthy and unbearable, just as they do their fellow misers.

The heart can also be treated by thinking about the purposes for which money was created, and by not keeping any more of it than [a person] needs. The rest, he should store away for himself [so to speak] by obtaining the reward that comes from distributing it freely.

These antidotes come from knowledge and understanding. If [a person] comes to understand through the light of insight that distributing his money is better for him than holding onto it both in [this] world and in the next, it will spark his desire to use his money to benefit others. Then, when the occasion presents itself, he should respond to his initial impulse [to help] and not hesitate, remembering that Satan threatens him with poverty in an attempt to frighten him and prevent him [from acting].

> One day, Abū al-Ḥasan al-Būshanjī was answering the call of nature [when he realized that a poor man he knew was in need of a shirt].
>
> So, he called one of his students and said, "Take my shirt off and give it to so-and-so."
>
> "Perhaps you should wait until you have finished what you are doing?" he [his student] suggested.
>
> To this he [Abū al-Ḥasan] replied, "Now that I've thought of giving it away, I don't trust myself not to change my mind."[2]

2 Narrated by al-Qushayrī in his *Risālah* (420).

The quality of miserliness can only be uprooted by forcing oneself to give money away, just as romantic passion can only be overcome
by forcing oneself to leave the object of one's passion and traveling 216
to a distant enough place, then enduring patiently for a time until one's heart finds consolation [in other things]. Similarly, whoever wants the remedy for miserliness must force himself to part with his money by giving it away.

Indeed, it would be better for whoever has a fierce love of money to throw it into the sea than to continue holding onto it.[3]

A subtle trick [to employ in the uprooting of miserliness] is for [a person] to think about the name he might make for himself as a person of great generosity, in which case he will find it easier to give away his money in order to show off before others, until he becomes generous out of a desire to be seen as openhanded. In so doing, he rid himself of the vice of miserliness by cultivating the vice of ostentation. After this, however, he also tends to ostentation with its [respective] remedy. Thus, we find consolation in the pursuit of a good reputation as we wean ourselves away from money, just as a baby is consoled while being weaned off the breast by being allowed to play with sparrows and other things. The purpose here is not the play itself, but rather to shift the child's attention from the mother's breast to other things. In short, we pit one aberrant trait against another, the way lust is pitted against anger as a way of breaking its violent force, or the way anger is pitted against lust as a way of reining in its recklessness.

This approach is helpful for people whose miserliness has more power over them than their love for prestige and fame, since the more
powerful [vice] is replaced by the less powerful one. However, in the 217
case of someone for whom fame is as beloved to him as is money,

3 Amazed at this statement, Ibn al-Qayyim said, "All jurists agree that it is unlawful to throw money into the sea." In response to this, we say: Those who travel the spiritual path use their personal judgment to reach conclusions about the various states they experience. Furthermore, one of the rules set down by scholars of the law is that in the face of two harms, we should avoid the greater of the two, even if this means committing the lesser of two harmful acts. The two harms being weighed in this situation are: corrupting one's spiritual integrity [by clinging to money out of sheer love for it], and doing damage to an earthly blessing [by throwing one's money in the sea]. And God knows best. See *Itḥāf* (1:38).

this approach will have no benefit, since now we will have done away with one malady only to reinforce another like it. If someone has no difficulty parting with money for the sake of appearances, it will be clear that ostentation has more power over the person than does the love of money. If, by contrast, parting with money brings hardship even though it helps to improve a person's image, he should give [the money away], since this indicates that the malady of miserliness has the most power over his heart.

An example of the way in which these qualities work against each other can be seen in the belief that all parts of a dead body eventually turn to worms, after which the worms consume each other, causing their numbers to decrease while they increase in size. They then continue to consume each other until only two powerful ones remain. These two remaining worms fight until one of them vanquishes and consumes the other, leaving only one. This single worm then remains alone with nothing to feed on until it starves to death. Similarly, these insidious qualities can be pitted against one another. The weaker become prey for the more powerful until only one remains, after which the Divine Providence and exertion [by the individual] wipe out [the vice] by denying it nourishment.

In order to thrive, a quality requires nourishment; otherwise, it will die out. So, [a person] denies a quality the nourishment it needs by not acting on it. Take the case of miserliness, for example, whose survival requires that [the person] hold onto their wealth. If he refuses to nourish it, relinquishing his wealth repeatedly and with conscious effort, the quality of miserliness will die out. As a result, relinquishing freely will become second-nature and no longer cause him any hardship.

Hence, the remedy for miserliness lies in both knowledge and action. On the level of knowledge, one needs to understand what a harm miserliness is, as well as the benefits of openhandedness. And on the level of action, one needs to consistently force oneself to be openhanded and let one's money go, [walking] along the path of
218 constraint. However, miserliness can take root and grow so powerful that it renders us blind and deaf to its deadly harms. Without the requisite understanding, there will be no desire to change; as a consequence, it will be difficult to act, and the affliction will remain

chronic. In this way, [miserliness] resembles an illness that prevents one from knowing its requisite medicine and how to use it, in the face of which there is nothing to do but wait patiently for death.

When treating the affliction of miserliness in their disciples, it was the custom of some Sufi shaykhs to forbid them to be attached to a single *zawiya*. If the shaykh noticed that a disciple of his was particularly happy with his *zawiya* and the things he found there, he would transfer him to someone else's *zawiya*, and transfer [the disciple of] someone else's *zawiya* to him, thereby separating [the disciple] from everything he possessed. Similarly, if he noticed that a certain disciple was paying special attention to a new robe he was wearing, or to a prayer carpet he was especially pleased with, [the shaykh] would instruct him to give it to someone else, and have him wear a tattered robe for which his heart had no predilection. Through [disciplines such as these], the heart develops an indifference to the things of [this] world. If [a person] does not follow this path, his fondness for [this] world will grow. If he has a thousand possessions, he will also have a thousand beloveds. If they are stolen from him, he will be afflicted by disaster, and the greater his love for them, the more terrible the disaster will be. Similarly when he dies, he will be afflicted by a thousand calamities at once. Indeed, throughout his life he will be in danger of disaster through poverty and [spiritual] perdition.

> A certain king was once gifted a turquoise goblet inlaid with precious jewels, the likes of which had never been seen.
>
> Overjoyed, the king asked one of his sages what he thought of the goblet.
>
> The sage replied, "I think it will spell disaster or poverty."
>
> "How is that?" asked the king.
>
> "If it is broken," he said, "it will be a disaster. If it is stolen, you will feel poverty-stricken without it, and you will never find any other like it, whereas before it was brought to you, you were safe from both disaster and poverty."
>
> Then one day, the goblet happened to break.
>
> Sorely stricken over the disaster, the king said, "The 219
> sage spoke truly. If only it had never been brought to us."

And thus it is with all worldly entities. [This] world is an enemy to the enemies of God, since it leads them to the fire. It is an enemy to the friends of God, since it burdens them with the struggle to forbear it. And it is an enemy to God, as it blocks His servants' path to Him. Indeed, it is its own enemy, since it consumes itself. After all, wealth can only be preserved and protected in safes and under guard, while safes and guards can only be obtained with wealth, that is, by spending dirhams and dinars. So, money consumes itself, acting against itself until it is annihilated. Whoever recognizes the harm of wealth will find neither consolation nor joy in it, and will not take more than the amount he needs. Whoever is satisfied with the amount he needs will not cling [to wealth]. He will only hold onto what he needs to cover his requirements and not out of miserliness. That which he does not require, he will not trouble himself trying to safeguard. Instead, he will let it go. This [surplus wealth] is like the water on the banks of the Tigris, which no one is miserly with, since it satisfies all people with the amount they need.

***

13

An Elucidation of the Rules to be Kept in Relation to One's Wealth 220

KNOW that based on our description of wealth thus far, it is good in one respect, and evil in another. Wealth might be likened to a viper which a healer seizes in order to extract its venom as an antidote, but which a heedless person might seize, only to be unexpectedly killed by its venom.

The only way in which anyone can protect themself from money's deadly venom is to observe five rules.

The first [rule] is to understand the purpose of wealth, why it was created, and that for which [a person] requires it, so as to avoid obtaining or keeping it, except for the amount he needs, and to avoid giving it more importance than it deserves.

***

The second [rule] is to be aware of the source from which [a person] obtains wealth so that he can avoid those sources which are utterly or even largely unlawful, such as wealth that comes from rulers, as well as disliked (*makrūh*) sources that would compromise his integrity, such as gifts that smack of bribery, and such as through begging, which is demeaning and in violation of his integrity, or anything else of this nature.

***

The third [rule] has to do with the amount acquired. He should seek to acquire neither too much nor too little, but rather, the requisite amount. The criterion for determining the requisite amount is his need, with "need" being clothing, shelter, and food, each of which
221 has three levels: lowest, medium, and highest. Those who tend to acquire and own only the bare necessities are classified as abstemious. Anything more than this will cause one to fall into a bottomless abyss. The details of these [three] levels are discussed in *The Book on* [*Poverty and*] *Abstinence*.

***

The fourth [rule] is to consider where his money goes and to be moderate in his spending, being neither extravagant nor tightfisted, as we have noted. The aim is to place what he has acquired by lawful means in its lawful place, and nowhere else. Just as it is a sin to acquire money from an unlawful source, so also is it a sin to spend it in an unlawful manner.

***

And the fifth [rule] is to ensure that [a person's] intention in acquiring or letting go, spending or withholding, is pure, so that he acquires what he acquires in order to facilitate his worship, and that he releases what he releases out of genuine self-denial (*zuhd*) and contempt for [the wealth he releases]. If he does this, having wealth will not harm him.

For this reason, ʿAlī رَضِيَ ٱللَّهُ عَنْهُ said, "If a person acquired all the riches in the world and intended to seek God's سُبْحَانَهُ وَتَعَالَىٰ favor with them, he would be abstinent (*zāhid*). Conversely, if he spurned all the riches in the world but did not do so in pursuit of God's سُبْحَانَهُ وَتَعَالَىٰ favor, he would not be abstinent."

***

So, whether you are at rest or in motion, let all you do be for God سُبْحَانَهُ وَتَعَالَىٰ: for the sole purpose of worship or to that which supports worship. The actions of eating and eliminating bodily wastes are
222 as far as can be from acts of worship. However, they help to enable worship, and if this is your intention behind engaging in them, then they will be counted as worship for you. Your intention should be

similar in relation to everything you keep, be it a shirt, a loincloth, a mattress, or utensils of some sort, since any of these items might be needed in [the practice of] the *dīn*. As for those items that are not so needed, they should be intended to benefit some servant of God, and they must not be denied to those who need them. Those who conduct themselves in this manner are like the person who extracts the essential substance and antidote from the viper of wealth while avoiding its venom. People such as these will not be harmed by an abundance of wealth. However, this will only come about to those who have firmly and knowledgeably planted their feet in the *dīn*. As for the unschooled who [merely] emulate those with knowledge and accumulate as much wealth as possible while claiming to be like the wealthy Companions, they are like the boy who, after seeing a skilled sorcerer handling a viper and extracting its antidote, imitates [the sorcerer], thinking that he merely picked up the viper because of its pleasing appearance and shape and its smooth skin, but is killed instantly. However, whereas the person killed by the viper realizes he is being killed, those who are killed by wealth may not be aware of it.

Likening [this] world to a viper, someone once said:

> Like a viper, [this] world spews venom,
> though it be soft to the touch.[1]

Just as the blind could not emulate those who see in traversing mountain summits, maritime expanses, and thorny paths, neither can the unschooled emulate one with full knowledge in the proper handling of wealth.

***

1 From the *dīwān* of Abū al-ʿAtāhiya (75).

14

223 An Elucidation of the Censure of Affluence (*al-ghinā*) and the Praise of Poverty (*al-faqr*)

KNOW that people have differed over whether those who are affluent and grateful are to be preferred over those who are poor and long-suffering, a topic we examined in *The Book on Poverty and Abstinence*, wherein we unveiled the full truth [on the matter].

In this book, by contrast, we show that poverty is preferable to, and higher in rank than affluence, without going into specific details [which were covered in the other book].

We will limit ourselves to a story in a book entitled *al-Radd ʿalā baʿḍ al-ʿulamāʾ al-aghniyāʾ* [In rebuttal of a certain wealthy scholar] by al-Ḥārith al-Muḥāsibī رَضِيَ اللَّهُ عَنْهُ. Here, [al-Muḥāsibī] refers to a certain scholar who likened himself to the affluent among the Companions [in an attempt to justify his own wealth], appealing [specifically] to the example of the wealth of ʿAbd al-Raḥmān b. ʿAwf رَضِيَ اللَّهُ عَنْهُ. Al-Mūḥāsibī رَحِمَهُ اللَّهُ was the foremost Islamic scholar of what one might term spiritual ethics (*ʿilm al-muʿāmala*).[1] He was a leading researcher of human flaws, the harms posed by human actions, and the deeper meanings of rites of worship. Hence, what he has to say is worth quoting directly.

***

1 MS 'j' uses the phrase *khayr al-umma* ('the best of the community of [Muslims]') instead of *ḥabr al- umma* ('the most learned scholar of the community of [Muslims]').

After writing a rebuttal of scholars of ill intent, [al- Ḥārith al-Muḥāsibī] added,

> We have been told that Jesus عَلَيْهِ ٱلسَّلَامُ said, "O scholars of
> ill intent, you fast, you perform the ritual prayers, and
> you distribute alms. However, you do not do what you are
> commanded, and you teach others what you yourselves
> do not do. How poorly you judge! You repent with mere 224
> words and wishes, while acting on the basis of your selfish
> whims. It will not benefit you to you refine your outward
> appearances when your hearts are defiled.
>
> "Truly I say to you, be not like the sieve, which yields fine flour while holding the bran and husk inside it. Thus it is that words of wisdom come out of your mouths, while malice roils in your breasts.
>
> "O slaves of [this] world, how do you expect to enjoy the hereafter when your lust for [this] world is never satisfied, your craving for it never sated?!
>
> "Truly I say to you, your hearts weep over the things you do, for [this world] is frequently on your tongues and you trample [good] works underfoot.
>
> "Truly I say to you, you have ruined your hereafter, for you would prefer to excel in [this] world rather than excel in the hereafter. You are the greatest of losers, if you but knew!
>
> "Woe to you! How long will you go on claiming to show the way to those who seek God, all the while remaining confounded yourselves, as though you were calling on the inhabitants of [this] world to leave its blessings to you? Think twice about what you do and say.[2]
>
> "Woe to you! What good will it do a dark house for a lamp to be placed on its roof while the structure remains gloomy and dark within? And neither will it do you any good for the light of knowledge to fill your mouths while being absent from your inward beings.

---

2 The account as it appears in *al-Waṣāyā* (75) replaces the word *al-mutaḥayyirīn* (translated above as "confounded") with *al-mutaḥabbirīn* ("those who compose elegant and scholarly writings").

"O slaves to [this] world, being neither God-fearing
225 slaves nor noble free people, [this] world is about to uproot you and cast you on your faces, then fling you on your noses. Your faults will then seize you by your forelocks as knowledge pushes you from behind and delivers you naked and alone to the King and Judge, who will call you to account for your disgraceful actions and recompense you for the evil of your deeds."[3]

***

Al-Ḥārith [al-Muḥāsibī] رَحِمَهُ ٱللَّهُ then wrote:

Brothers, these are scholars of ill intent, demons of the human race, and a tribulation for other people. They desire the honors of [this] world and exalted status within it, preferring these things to the hereafter, and subjecting matters of the *dīn* to [this] world. In this present time, they are a shame and a disgrace, and in the hereafter, they will be the losers unless the Most Gracious should choose in His bounty to pardon.

I have seen how the merriment of those who are perishing, having preferred [this] world [over the hereafter], is mingled with distress, out of which erupts all manner of worries and acts of disobedience. They are destined for destruction and perdition. Hence, the joy of those whose perishing will turn to sorrow, for [this] world is no longer theirs, while their *dīn* has not been sound. They have lost both [this] world and the hereafter, which is the most manifest loss.

What a great disaster there is in their hideousness! I urge you, brothers: Be mindful of God. Do not allow Satan and those who submit to him to deceive you with arguments
226 that will hold no weight before God. For they vie with one another for [this] world, then offer [flimsy] excuses and arguments for themselves [before God], claiming that the Companions of the Messenger of God صَلَّى ٱللَّهُ عَلَيْهِ وَسَلَّمَ possessed

3 Most of Jesus's statements about our Prophet صَلَّى ٱللَّهُ عَلَيْهِ وَسَلَّمَ were included by Ibn ʿAsākir in *Tārīkh Dimashq* (68:59, 47:460).

wealth. Such self-deceived individuals attempt to put on a pleasant face [to cover their greed] by making mention of the Companions, hoping that people will excuse them for amassing wealth, and not realizing that Satan has led them astray.

Woe be to you, O you who have been dazzled! Your argument based on the wealth of ʿAbd al-Raḥmān b. ʿAwf is a ruse of Satan which he has placed on your tongue, in order to cause you to perish. For when you claim that the purest of the Companions desired wealth in order to amass riches, increase in rank, and enjoy the adornments of [this] world, you slander those who are spiritual leaders and attribute to them something awful indeed!

When you claim that it is higher and better to amass lawful wealth than to abstain from it, you belittle Muḥammad صَلَّى ٱللَّهُ عَلَيْهِ وَسَلَّمَ and other messengers, since you imply that they were ignorant for not desiring, and abstaining from, the blessing that you and your friends so desire when you amass wealth for yourselves. They did not amasss wealth as you do!

When you claim that amassing lawful wealth is superior to refraining from it, this is tantamount to the claim that the Messenger of God صَلَّى ٱللَّهُ عَلَيْهِ وَسَلَّمَ did not give wise counsel to the community [of Muslims], that he forbade them from amassing wealth while [supposedly] knowing that [doing so] is beneficial for them. But, rather, cheated them—or so you claim—by forbidding them to amass wealth. By the Lord of the heavens, you lie about the Messenger of God صَلَّى ٱللَّهُ عَلَيْهِ وَسَلَّمَ! For, in fact, he was the best of counselors to the community [of Muslims], being compassionate and merciful to them.

When you claim that amassing wealth is preferable [to not doing so], you are claiming that God سُبْحَانَهُ وَتَعَالَىٰ did not
have His servants' best interests at heart when He forbade 227
them to amass wealth, since He [supposedly] knew full well that to do so would actually have been better for them. Alternatively, you are claiming that when God سُبْحَانَهُ وَتَعَالَىٰ forbade His people to amass wealth, He did so without

knowing the blessing it would be for them, whereas you yourself know of its benefits and for this reason you want to accumulate huge sums of it. Hence, you claim to know where the good lies better than your Lord does—exalted be God سُبْحَانَهُ وَتَعَالَىٰ over your ignorance!

O deluded souls! Think carefully about the deception of Satan to which you fell prey when he lured you into arguing on the basis of the wealth owned by the Companions. Woe to you! What do you gain from citing the example of ʿAbd al-Raḥmān b. ʿAwf who himself wished, [in anticipation of] the day of resurrection, that all he had received from [this] world was his daily sustenance?

I have heard [the following]:

When ʿAbd al-Raḥmān b. ʿAwf رَضِيَ ٱللَّهُ عَنْهُ died, other Companions of the Messenger of God صَلَّى ٱللَّهُ عَلَيْهِ وَسَلَّمَ said, "We fear for ʿAbd al-Raḥmān on account of what he left behind."

In response, Kaʿb said, "Glory be to God! Why do you fear for ʿAbd al-Raḥmān? He earned what was good. He spent it in good ways. And he left what was good."

When word of what Kaʿb had said reached Abū Dharr, he went out angrily looking for Kaʿb. Coming across a camel's dried jaw bone, he picked it up and set out in Kaʿb's pursuit. When Kaʿb was told that Abū Dharr was after him, he fled to the home of ʿUthmān رَضِيَ ٱللَّهُ عَنْهُ [who was caliph at the time] seeking his protection, and told him what had happened. Abū Dharr followed Kaʿb to ʿUthmān's house رَضِيَ ٱللَّهُ عَنْهُ. When Abū Dharr entered, Kaʿb got up and hid behind ʿUthmān.

Abū Dharr said to Kaʿb, "Come on now, tell me, you son of a Jewish woman, are you claiming that there is nothing wrong with what ʿAbd al-Raḥmān b. ʿAwf left when he died? [Then listen to the following:]

The Messenger of God صَلَّى ٱللَّهُ عَلَيْهِ وَسَلَّمَ set out one day toward Uḥud, and I was with him.

'Abū Dharr?' he said.

'I am at your service, O Messenger of God,' I replied.

And he said, 'On the day of resurrection, [those who possessed] the most will [possess] the least,[4] except for
those who distributed their wealth this way and that, to 228
their right and to their left, before them and behind them. But they will be few.' Then he said, 'Abū Dharr?'

I replied, 'Yes, O Messenger of God, precious to me as my father and my mother.'

He said, 'I would not want to have a pile of gold the size of Mt. Uḥud that I could spend in the cause of God if it meant that I would die one day leaving [even so much as] two kerats[5] of it behind.'

I asked, 'Or [perhaps you mean] two kantars,[6] O Messenger of God?'

'No, two kerats,' he insisted. 'You, Abū Dharr, want it to be more, and I want it to be less!'

[Abū Dharr concluded by saying], "This is how the Messenger of God felt about such matters, yet here you are, you son of a Jewish woman, saying there was no problem with what was left by ʿAbd al-Raḥmān b. ʿAwf?! You lie, and so does anyone who says as much."

Then [Kaʿb] left without making any reply.[7]

---

4 Trans.: This is because, distracted and burdened inwardly by their wealth, the rich are often lulled into a false sense of self-sufficiency, which engenders arrogance and an indifference to worship and obedience to God. Therefore, they will have little to speak for them before God on the day of judgment.

5 Trans.: A kerat is a unit of weight equal to 0.195 grams.

6 Trans.: A kantar is a unit of weight that varies widely, from 44.93 kg in Egypt to 256.4 kg in Syria.

7 The prophetic *ḥadīth* that formed part of the statement by al-Ḥārith رحمه الله was narrated by al-Bukhārī (6444) and Muslim (94), the Book of *Zakāt*, the section entitled, *bāb al-targhīb fi-l-ṣadaqa* [the chapter on incentives to giving alms]. The encounter between Abū Dharr and ʿUthmān رضي الله عنهما and their conversation about ʿAbd al-Raḥmān b. ʿAwf رضي الله عنه was narrated by Aḥmad in his *Musnad* (1:63), where we are told that Abū Dharr came asking ʿUthmān b. ʿAffān رضي الله عنه for permission [to enter his home]. So, he granted him permission, and he [Abū Dharr] had a stick in his hand. "O Kaʿb," said ʿUthmān رضي الله عنه, "ʿAbd al-Raḥmān b. ʿAwf died leaving money. What do you think about that?" To this Kaʿb replied, "If the money reached [his kin, then this was] a duty to God, and there was nothing wrong with it." Abū Dharr then raised his stick and struck Kaʿb, saying, "I once heard the Messenger of God صلى الله عليه وسلم say, 'I would not want to have this mountain's weight in gold to

We have heard that ʿAbd al-Raḥmān b. ʿAwf once received a caravan from Yemen, which set the whole city in an uproar.

"What is this?" asked ʿĀʾisha رَضِيَ اللَّهُ عَنْهَا.

Someone replied saying, "It's a caravan that's arrived for ʿAbd al-Raḥmān."

She said, "God and His Messenger of God صَلَّى اللَّهُ عَلَيْهِ وَسَلَّمَ spoke truly."

When this reached ʿAbd al-Raḥmān, he asked her [about it], and she explained, "I once heard the Messenger of God صَلَّى اللَّهُ عَلَيْهِ وَسَلَّمَ say, 'I had a vision of the garden in which I saw the poverty-stricken Emigrants and other poor Muslims
229 entering it at a lively pace. I saw no wealthy person among them with the exception of ʿAbd al-Raḥmān b. ʿAwf, and him I saw entering it crawling.'"

And ʿAbd al-Raḥmān said, "I hereby declare the caravan and everything in it to be devoted to the cause of God, and its slaves are hereby released. I hope now that I might enter the garden with them, running at full speed."[8]

We have heard that the Prophet صَلَّى اللَّهُ عَلَيْهِ وَسَلَّمَ said to ʿAbd al-Raḥmān b. ʿAwf, "You are the first of the wealthy of my community [of Muslims] to enter the garden, yet you barely entered on your knees."[9]

Woe to you, deluded souls! What is this argument of yours in favor of wealth when ʿAbd al-Raḥmān b. ʿAwf, with all his virtue and God-fearing piety, all his good deeds, all the money he spent in the cause of God, his companionship with the Messenger of God صَلَّى اللَّهُ عَلَيْهِ وَسَلَّمَ, and his having received

---

spend in the way of God, even if it were going to be accepted from me, if I knew I would strew behind me [even] six ounces.' Swear by God, ʿUthmān: Did you hear him?" [He repeated his question] three times, whereupon [ʿUthmān] replied, "Yes, I heard him."

8 Narrated by Aḥmad in *al-Musnad* (6:115) without mentioning the poor Emigrants and other Muslims.

9 Narrated by al-Ḥākim in *al-Mustadrak* (3:311) and by al-Bayhaqī in *al-Shuʿab* (3064), where it reads, "O Son of ʿAwf, you are wealthy, and you will only enter the garden on your knees ..." Similarly, Abū Nuʿaym cited a version in *Faḍāʾil al-khulafāʾ al-rāshidīn* [Virtues of the rightly-guided caliphs] (119) from the *ḥadīth* of Anas رَضِيَ اللَّهُ عَنْهُ which reads, "The first wealthy person to enter the garden was ʿAbd al-Raḥmān b. ʿAwf."

the glad tidings that he would be among those admitted to the garden,[10] was stopped on the day of resurrection itself in the midst of all its horrors because of money he had earned by lawful means and with the intention of abstaining from spending it on himself? [This despite] his good deeds: that he had spent his money in an intentional manner, and he had given in abundance in the cause of God. [Even then,] he was forbidden to approach the garden running with the poor Emigrants, but rather, had to crawl in after them! So, what do you suppose will happen to people like us who are immersed in the tribulations of [this] world?!

I marvel at those deluded souls that revel in the deliria 230
(*takhālīṭ*) of things that are questionable (*al-shubhāt*) and illegal (*al-suḥt*), who rush into [engagement with] the filthiest aspects in people, all the while steeped in lusts, vainglory, and infatuation with worldly adornment, moving from one worldly tribulation to another, only then to seek justification in the life of ʿAbd al-Raḥmān b. ʿAwf. You argue that if you have amassed wealth, then so did the Prophet's Companions, as though you were following in the footsteps of the [righteous] predecessors. Woe to you! This kind of comparison is inspired by Satan, and is from the temptations [devised] for his followers.

[In what follows] I will describe your conditions, and those of the [righteous] predecessors, so that you might perceive your vices [by contrast], and the virtues of the Companions.

Truly I tell you: Some of the Companions possessed wealth which they desired not for their own sake, but to spend it in the cause of God. As such, they earned money through lawful means, they consumed what they needed with enjoyment and appreciation, they spent their money in a conscious, intentional manner, and they gave to others what exceeded their requirements. They never refused to

---

10 The Prophet's صَلَّى ٱللَّهُ عَلَيْهِ وَسَلَّمَ announcement to ʿAbd al-Raḥmān b. ʿAwf رَضِيَ ٱللَّهُ عَنْهُ that he would enter the garden along with nine other Companions was recorded by Abū Dāwūd (4649) and al-Tirmidhī (3748). Al-Ghazālī رَحِمَهُ ٱللَّهُ also cited other *ḥadīth*s in this connection.

place it where it was needed, nor did they withhold it. On the contrary, they shared most of it in God's service, and some of them shared all they had. In times of hardship they regularly preferred God over themselves. Heavens above! Are you this way? You most certainly bear no resemblance to these upright individuals!

The most righteous of the Companions had a love for modesty and simplicity. Rather than fearing poverty, they trusted in God for their daily sustenance. They were content with what God had allotted to each of them, uncomplaining in affliction, thankful in times of plenty, full of praise in good times, and patient in bad. They were humble before their Lord and wary of a fondness for elevated status and the accumulation of wealth. They sought nothing of [this] world but that which would be permitted to them, contenting themselves with bare sufficiency. They spurned [this] world and patiently bore its adversities, drank of its bitterness, and abstained from its comforts and luxuries. Again: Are these [the virtues] you claim for yourself?

231 We have received reports according to which, if earthly fortune came their way, they [the righteous predecessors] would grieve, saying, "We must have committed some sin for which God's سُبْحَانَهُ وَتَعَالَىٰ punishment has been hastened.' If, on the other hand, they saw poverty approaching, they would say, 'Welcome to the badge of the righteous!"[11]

We have received reports according to which a certain man, if he woke in the morning to find that his family had something, would be despondent, and if they had nothing, he would rejoice. Once he was asked, "Most people, if they have nothing, are despondent, and if they have something, they rejoice. But you are not like this." He replied, "If, when I wake in the morning, my family has nothing, I rejoice, because I am emulating the example of Muḥammad

11 In *al-Ḥilya* (6:5), Abū Nuʿaym narrates on the authority of Kaʿb, "The Lord سُبْحَانَهُ وَتَعَالَىٰ once said to Moses عَلَيْهِ ٱلسَّلَامُ, 'O Moses, if you see wealth approaching, say: I must have committed some sin for which God's سُبْحَانَهُ وَتَعَالَىٰ punishment has been hastened. And if you see poverty approaching, say: Welcome to the badge of the righteous." This was also cited earlier.

صَلَّى ٱللَّهُ عَلَيْهِ وَسَلَّمَ. If, on the other hand, my family has something, I am distressed, since I am not emulating the example set down by the family of Muḥammad صَلَّى ٱللَّهُ عَلَيْهِ وَسَلَّمَ."

Similarly, we have been told that if they were taken onto the path of prosperity, they would grow despondent and fearful, saying, "What do we want with [this] world and its purposes?" It is as if they perched on the edge [literally, 'wing'] of fear. If, by contrast, they were led onto the path of tribulation, they would rejoice and take heart, saying, "Now our Lord has kept his covenant with us."

Such were the spiritual states and characters of the [righteous] predecessors, who also possessed other virtues that we have not described here. Good God, are you this way?! You are a far cry from [those upright] people.

O deluded souls, I shall now describe your spiritual states, which are in complete contrast to those of the [righteous predecessors]. For when riches come your way, you become tyrants. When you are prosperous, you turn reckless. Good
fortune makes you rejoice, and you neglect to thank your 232
Divine Benefactor for what you have been given. You fall into despair in times of ill-fortune, and in affliction, you turn resentful. You are not content with God's decrees for you. You abhor poverty and you hold humility in disdain, considering yourself above it, though it was the pride and joy of [God's] messengers. You amass and hoard money for fear of falling into poverty, which means that you think ill of God عَزَّ وَجَلَّ, not trusting in His provision for you. [These attitudes] in themselves are a kind of sin.

Perhaps you save up money in hopes of enjoying [this] world's comforts and splendor, [indulging in] your desires and worldly pleasures. We have heard that the Messenger of God صَلَّى ٱللَّهُ عَلَيْهِ وَسَلَّمَ said, "The villains of my community [of Muslims] are those who have fed on ease, and whose bodies have grown accustomed to it."[12]

---

12 Narrated by Ibn Abī al-Dunyā in *al-Ṣamt wa Ādāb al-Lisān* [Silence and the etiquette of the tongue] (150), by Ibn ʿAdī in *al-Kāmil* (5:318) from a *ḥadīth* of Lady Fāṭima

A certain person of knowledge once said, "On the day of resurrection, some people will come looking for rewards. And they will be told, *You exhausted your pleasures during your worldly life and enjoyed them* [Q. 46:20]. Without realizing it, you have been deprived of the bliss of the hereafter due to the bliss you enjoyed in [this] world. What a disaster and cause for regret!"

Yes, and perhaps you save up money in hopes of prosperity, exalted status, a reason to be proud, and an attractive appearance in [this] world. However, we have learned that those who seek the things of [this] world for the sake of mere accumulation or a reason to boast will find God wrathful against them on the day of resurrection.[13] Hence, when you seek to accumulate for the sake of accumulation and pursue exalted status in [this] world, you are demonstrating your indifference to the wrath of God that awaits you.

233 Yes. Perhaps you would rather remain in [this] world than go to be near God سُبْحَانَهُ وَتَعَالَىٰ? If the idea of meeting God is odious to you, then it is more odious still to God. You are in a state of heedlessness.

Perhaps you regret worldly opportunities that have passed you by. However, we have learned that the Messenger of God صَلَّى ٱللَّٰهُ عَلَيْهِ وَسَلَّمَ said, "Those who sorrow over a worldly good that has been lost come closer to the fire by the distance of one month's march." (And some versions read, "of a year's [march]."[14]) So, when you sigh in regret over what

---

رَضِيَ ٱللَّٰهُ عَنْهَا, by al-Ṭabarānī in *al-Kabīr* (8:107), and by Abū Nuʿaym in *al-Ḥilya* (6:90) from a *ḥadīth* of Abū Umāma رَضِيَ ٱللَّٰهُ عَنْهُ.

13 Narrated by Ibn Abī Shayba in *al-Muṣannaf* (22625), by Ibn Abī al-Dunyā in *al-ʿIyāl* (32), by Abū Nuʿaym in *al-Ḥilya* (3:109), and by al-Bayhaqī in *al-Shuʿab* (9890) from a *ḥadīth* of Abū Hurayra رَضِيَ ٱللَّٰهُ عَنْهُ.

14 Al-Ḥāfiẓ al-ʿIrāqī said, "We narrated it in the book entitled *al-Qurba* by Abū Ḥafṣ al-ʿAtkī from the account of ʿAmr b. Shuʿayb on the authority of his father, who heard it from his own father, according to whom it read, 'by the distance one could travel in one thousand years (*masīrata alfi sana*).'" Its chain of transmission is weak. In this connection we cited it in Part 12 of al-Khalʿī's work entitled, *al-Fawāʾid*. See *Itḥāf* (8:219). It is cited by al-Muttaqī al-Hindī in *Kanz al-ʿUmmāl* (6147), where he attributes it to al-Rāzī in his *Mashyakha* on the authority of Ibn ʿUmar رَضِيَ ٱللَّٰهُ عَنْهُمَا.

you have lost, you show disregard for how close you are to God's punishment.

Perhaps you leave off attending to your religious duties at times in order to provide for your worldly needs, and perhaps you rejoice when worldly blessings come your way, finding this to be a relief and a source of pleasure. We have learned that the Messenger of God صَلَّى ٱللَّٰهُ عَلَيْهِ وَسَلَّمَ said, "Whoever loves [this] world and its enjoyment, the fear of the hereafter leaves his heart."[15]

A certain person of knowledge is reported to have said, "You shall be called to account for the times when you grieved over worldly fortunes lost, just as you shall be called to account for the times when you rejoiced over worldly fortunes enjoyed. For when you rejoice in your worldly fortunes, you have been stripped of your fear of God سُبْحَانَهُ وَتَعَالَىٰ."

Perhaps you concern yourself with affairs of this world 234
far more than you do with your affairs pertaining to the hereafter.

Perhaps you view the disaster you will suffer due to your acts of disobedience as less distressing than the disaster you suffer at loss of worldly things. Indeed, your fear of losing your wealth is greater than your fear of wrongdoing.

Perhaps what you give to others from what you have accumulated of tainted wealth, you give simply in order to elevate your worldly station and rank, seeking honor and recognition from other creatures through acts that are odious to God سُبْحَانَهُ وَتَعَالَىٰ. Woe to you! It seems that being despised by God سُبْحَانَهُ وَتَعَالَىٰ on the day of resurrection is a less frightful to you than being despised by people.

Perhaps you conceal your faults from other creatures while giving little thought to God's knowledge of them, as though being exposed before God سُبْحَانَهُ وَتَعَالَىٰ is less frightful to you than being exposed before other people. It seems that

15 Narrated by Ibn Abī al-Dunyā in *al-Zuhd* (169) on the authority of al-Ḥasan, by Abū Nuʿaym in al-*Ḥilya* (7:79) on the authority of Sufyān al-Thawrī. Al-Ḥāfiẓ al-ʿIrāqī said, "I have only found it in the form of a statement by al-Ḥārith b. Asad as mentioned by al-Ghazālī likewise on his authority." See *Itḥāf* (8:219).

slaves have a higher standing in your mind than does God Himself, God سُبْحَانَهُ وَتَعَالَىٰ be exalted over your ignorance!

How dare you speak in the presence of those with pure hearts when you are riddled with such faults? Fie on you! Polluted to the core, you argue that the righteous had wealth!

How far off the mark you are! What a chasm lies between you and the righteous predecessors! I swear to God, they were more abstemious in relation to what was lawful to them than you are in relation to what has been unlawful to you, and actions which are unobjectionable to you were viewed by them as terrible transgressions![16] They viewed a minor slip as a greater catastrophe than you do major disobediences. If only the most lawful and untainted of your possessions were as pure as the possessions they held in suspicion. If
235 only you feared your bad deeds as much as they feared that their good would not be accepted from them. If only your fasting were as virtuous as their fast-breaking. If only the effort you expend on worship were on a par with their moments of lethargy and sleep. If only all of your good deeds together amounted to a single good deed of theirs.

One of the Companions is reported to have said, "The spoils of the upright consist in what passed them by [that is, what they did not obtain] of [this] world, and their burning desire is for it [the spoils of this world] to remain concealed from them. Unless you adopt this same attitude, you will not be joined with [the upright] either in [this] world or in the next."

Glory be to God! What a vast difference there is between the two groups—between the best of the Companions, raised aloft with God, and those who, like you, remain in the depths of depravity[17]—unless the Generous One should choose in His bounty to pardon [you].

---

16 In *al-Qūt* (1:255), al-Ḥasan is quoted as having said, "I saw seventy of the men who fought at the Battle of Badr who were more abstemious in relation to what God سُبْحَانَهُ وَتَعَالَىٰ had permitted to them than you are in relation to what God سُبْحَانَهُ وَتَعَالَىٰ has forbidden to you."

17 Imam al-Muḥāsibī's wording reads, "a group with the best of the Companions ... and a group with the likes of them who are among the most debased."

Thus, if you claim to be emulating the Companions by amassing wealth in order simply to spend it in the cause of God, take a careful look at yourself. Woe to you! Will you find lawful [sources of wealth] in your times as they did in theirs? Do you truly believe you are as cautious as they were in your pursuit of that which is lawful?!

A certain Companion is reported to have said, "We would forego seventy types of lawful pleasures for fear of inadvertently doing one thing that was unlawful."[18] Do you aspire to be as cautious as this? I swear by the Lord of the Kaʿba, you do not!

Woe to you! You can be certain that collecting money, even for the purpose of righteous actions, is a ruse of Satan whose purpose is to lure you into committing dubious actions
tainted with the unlawful. The Messenger of God صَلَّى ٱللَّٰهُ عَلَيْهِ وَسَلَّمَ 236
said, "Those who dare to commit dubious acts (*al-shubhāt*) are in danger of falling into acts that are unlawful."[19]

O deceived souls: Do you not realize that your fear of engaging in dubious actions is higher, more virtuous, and greater for your standing before God than acquiring dubious income even if you spend it in the cause of God سُبْحَانَهُ وَتَعَالَىٰ and in the way of devotion? As a certain person of knowledge is reported to have said, "It would be better for you to abstain from a single dirham for fear of its not being lawful than to donate one thousand dinars in charity without questioning about whether it came from a lawful source or not."

If you claim to be too God-fearing and pious to be drawn into dubious means of acquiring income, insisting that, instead, you are making money lawfully in order to spend it in the cause of God سُبْحَانَهُ وَتَعَالَىٰ, woe to you! If you are as pious as you claim to be, then you will not be subjected to

18 Narrated by al-Qushayrī in his *Risāla* (210) on the authority of our master Abū Bakr the Most Righteous رَضِيَ ٱللَّٰهُ عَنْهُ.

19 A similar version is narrated by Muslim (1599), this version having been cited earlier, and by al-Bukhārī (2051), whose version reads, "Those who dare to engage in actions which they suspect of being sinful are on the verge of committing actions which are sinful without a doubt."

an accounting. For the most righteous of the Companions feared being [brought to account] before God.

As one Companion is reported to have said,

"I would not want to earn 1,000 dinars every day, [even it were] from a lawful source and [even if I were to] spend it in ways that demonstrate obedience to God, and even if such business did not prevent me from attending the Friday congregational prayer."

Someone asked, "And why is that, God have mercy on you?"

He replied, "Because on the day of resurrection, I do not want God to say: 'Tell me, My servant, where did you get [your money], and what did you spend it on?'"[20]

237 These God-fearing individuals lived in the early days of Islam, at which time there were truly lawful ways in which to earn an income. Nevertheless, they abandoned wealth, afraid of the account to which they would be subjected, and afraid that the goodness of wealth would not compensate for its evil. As for you, you are the most worthless members of the community [of Muslims]. There is nothing that might rightly be deemed lawful in your day and age. You run after worthless filth, then claim to be amassing wealth through lawful means. Woe to you! Where are there lawful earnings for you to amass?

Now, if there really were such a thing as lawful [money] for you to earn, would you not be afraid that upon becoming affluent, your heart would change? We have received reports to the effect that a certain Companion inherited lawful wealth,

20 In *al-Ḥilya* (1:209), Abū Nuʿaym narrated the following account on the authority of ʿAmr b. Murra: "Abū l-Dardāʾ once said, 'When the Prophet ﷺ was appointed to his prophetic mission, I was a merchant, and I wanted to combine commerce and worship. But this wasn't possible. So I abandoned commerce and began engaging only in worship. And I swear by the One who holds Abū l-Dardāʾ's soul in His hand: I do not like the fact that I now have a shop near the mosque entrance even though I never miss a prayer. Every day I make 40 dinars and I give it all away as alms in the service of God.' 'Abū l-Dardāʾ,' someone asked him, 'What is it that you don't like about this?' And he replied, 'The severe reckoning.'"

but declined [to accept] it for fear that it would corrupt his heart. Do you aspire to have a heart more God-fearing than the hearts of the Companions such that you never swerve from the truth in either your outward affairs or your spiritual states? If you think in this manner, then you have far too high an opinion of your lower self, which commands evil.

Woe to you! I advise you to be content with your basic necessities, and not to save money [even] for righteous works lest you be subjected to a severe reckoning. For we have received reports that the Messenger of God صَلَّى ٱللَّهُ عَلَيْهِ وَسَلَّمَ said, "Those whose accounts [before God] are subject to discussion … will be tormented."[21]

The Messenger of God صَلَّى ٱللَّهُ عَلَيْهِ وَسَلَّمَ also said: "On the day of resurrection, a man who amassed unlawful wealth and spent it in unlawful ways shall be brought [before the Throne], and it will be said, 'Away with him to the fire.' Then shall be brought a man who amassed lawful wealth which he spent in unlawful ways, and it will be said, 'Away with him to the fire.' Then shall be brought a man who amassed unlawful wealth which he spent in lawful ways, and it will 238
be said, 'Away with him to the fire.' Then shall be brought a man who amassed lawful wealth which he spent in lawful ways, and it will be said, 'Stop. Perhaps in the course of seeking this out, you neglected some of the duties I had imposed upon you. You may have failed to perform a ritual prayer at its appointed time. Or in the course of performing your prayer, you may have failed properly to perform a bow, a prostration, or an ablution.' In reply, he will say, 'No, O Lord, I earned lawful income, I spent it in lawful ways and I neglected none of the duties You had imposed upon me.' Then it will be said to him, 'Perhaps you took pride in this money or what it could buy—such as a mount or a robe of which you boasted.' And he will say, 'No, O Lord. I was not haughty, nor did I boast.' Then it will be said to him, 'Perhaps you neglected the rights of someone I had commanded you to assist—such as kinsfolk, orphans,

21 Narrated by al-Bukhārī (6536) and Muslim (2876).

the needy, and wayfarers.' And he will say, 'No, O Lord, I earned lawful income, and I spent it in lawful ways. And I neglected none of the duties You had imposed upon me. I did not grow haughty or boast. Nor did I neglect the right of any of those You had commanded me to give to.' Then the people to whom the man had been commanded to give will come forward and make their argument, saying, 'O Lord, You gave to him, You enriched him, You placed him in our midst, and You commanded him to give to us.' Then, if he had in fact given to these people without having neglected any of his religious duties, and if, moreover, he had not grown self-important or boastful, he will be told, 'Stop now, and give thanks for every blessing I bestowed upon you, be it food, drink, or enjoyment.' And he will still go on being questioned."[22]

Woe to you! Ponder well the reckoning that was faced by this man, who dealt only in that which was lawful, gave everyone their due, and performed all of his religious duties within their prescribed limits, yet was taken to task most severely. If this is the accounting to which a man of such virtue was subjected, then what awaits those who, like us, have lived our lives immersed in [this] world's tribulations
239 (*fitan*), its deliria (*takhālīṭ*), its dubious pursuits (*shubhāt*),
its selfish desires (*shahwāt*), and its finery (*zīna*)?!

Woe to you! In view of this reckoning, the God-fearing are fearful of being embroiled in [this] world. Consequently, they content themselves with what they need and no more, while performing various kinds of righteousness with the wealth they have earned. Therefore—woe be to you—I present you with these righteous souls as an example for you to emulate. If you refuse to do so, claiming that you are the pinnacle of piety and God-consciousness, that you only take money from lawful sources—or so you claim—in order to spend it in the cause of God, that you have never

22 This is how the account is presented by al-Muḥāsibī in *al-Waṣāyā* (86). Al-Ḥāfiẓ al-ʿIrāqī wrote, saying, "I have found no origin for this *ḥadīth* in its entirety." See *Ithāf* (8:221).

spent any of your honestly earned money on anything you should not have, that your heart has never strayed from what pleases God due to the influence of wealth, and that you have never displeased God, either in your most secret thoughts or in public—I say, if these descriptions apply to you (though they most certainly do not, woe to you), [even then] it would behoove you to content yourself with the bare necessities and hold yourself aloof from the wealthy lest, like them, you be stopped for questioning [before the Throne]. Vie instead, to be in the company of the Chosen One صَلَّى ٱللَّهُ عَلَيْهِ وَسَلَّمَ, those who are not stopped for interrogation and reckoning [on the day of resurrection]. For [your choices] will yield either well-being or ruin. The Messenger of God صَلَّى ٱللَّهُ عَلَيْهِ وَسَلَّمَ said, "The destitute Emigrants will enter the garden five hundred years before the wealthy ones."[23] He صَلَّى ٱللَّهُ عَلَيْهِ وَسَلَّمَ also said, "The poor among the believers will enter the garden before the wealthy ones, [where] they will eat and enjoy themselves while the others are on their knees. And God will say, 'Before you is my request: You were people's rulers and monarchs [on earth]. So, show me what you did with what I gave you.'"[24]

A certain person of knowledge is reported to have said, 240
"I would rather have been part of the first generation of Muslims with Muhammad صَلَّى ٱللَّهُ عَلَيْهِ وَسَلَّمَ and his band than have the choicest of blessings."[25]

---

23 Narrated by Abū Dāwūd (3666), whose version reads, "O company of destitute Emigrants, rejoice in the news of the perfect light you will enjoy on the day of resurrection. You will enter the garden half a day before the rich, this half a day being equal to five hundred years."

24 The full *ḥadīth* in this version was cited by al-Muḥāsibī in *al-Waṣāyā* (88). Al-Ḥāfiẓ al-ʿIrāqī stated, "I have found no origin for it." See *Ithāf* (8:222). It begins with his صَلَّى ٱللَّهُ عَلَيْهِ وَسَلَّمَ words, "Poor believers will enter the garden before wealthy ones." The same *ḥadīth* is cited by al-Tirmidhī (2354) with the addition of, "… half a day, this half a day being equal to five hundred years." In *al-Zuhd* (1648), Aḥmad narrated on the authority of Ḥasan, who said, "Princes and the wealthy shall be gathered and told, 'You were rulers of the Muslims and those possessed of wealth. Thus, I hold you to account for what you have.'"

25 Al-Ḥāfiẓ al-Zabīdī stated in his *Itḥāf* (8:222), "A similar version was narrated by the author of *al-Qūt* on the authority of Saʿīd b. ʿĀmir on the authority of Judhaym رَضِيَ ٱللَّهُ عَنْهُ."

O people, lead the race with those who have lightened their earthly loads, who are in the company of God's messengers, and who are fearful of falling behind and being cut off from the Messenger of God صَلَّى ٱللَّٰهُ عَلَيْهِ وَسَلَّمَ.

It has been reported that a certain Companion was thirsty and prayed for water. He then received a sip of water and honey. When he tasted it, he was choked with tears. After weeping and weeping, he wiped the tears from his face, but when he went to speak, he began weeping all over again.

When he started crying even more, someone asked him, "Is all this on account of this sip?"

He replied, "Yes. One day I was visiting the Messenger of God صَلَّى ٱللَّٰهُ عَلَيْهِ وَسَلَّمَ in his house with no one else present, when suddenly he began pushing [something] away from himself, saying, 'Be gone with you!'

'May my father and mother be your ransom!' I said to him. 'I see no one here! Who are you speaking to?'

And he replied, 'This world. It reared its head and pressed itself upon me, and said to me, "O Muḥammad, take me." So I said, "Be gone with you!" And it replied, "Although you may escape from me, Muḥammad, those who come after you will not."'

241 So, now I'm afraid this [world] has overtaken me, to cut me off from the Messenger of God صَلَّى ٱللَّٰهُ عَلَيْهِ وَسَلَّمَ."[26]

O people: These outstanding souls wept for fear of being cut off from the Messenger of God صَلَّى ٱللَّٰهُ عَلَيْهِ وَسَلَّمَ by a mere sip of something that was perfectly lawful to them.

Woe to you! Though you are surrounded by all manner of blessing and desires, indulging ill-gotten gains and dubious actions, still you entertain no fear of being thus cut off. Fie on you. How monumental is your ignorance!

---

26 Narrated by Ibn Abī al-Dunyā in *Dhamm al-Dunyā* [Censure of [this] world] (11), by al-Bazzār in his *Musnad* (44), by al-Ḥākim in *al-Mustadrak* (4:309), and by al-Bayhaqī in *al-Shuʿab* (10039). The person who related the incident was our master Abū Bakr the Righteous رَضِيَ ٱللَّٰهُ عَنْهُ.

Woe to you! If, on the day of resurrection, you fall behind the Messenger of God صَلَّى ٱللَّٰهُ عَلَيْهِ وَسَلَّمَ, Muḥammad the Chosen One, the angels and prophets will see horrors which will cause anxiety [even] for them. If you fall back in the race, you will be slow to catch up. If you desire too much, you will be destined for an arduous accounting. If you are not satisfied with little, you will be destined for a long wait and will be left weeping and wailing. If you are content to suffer the lot of those who fall behind, you will most surely be cut off from the Companions of the Right,[27] and from the Messenger of the Lord of the Worlds, and you will be slow to join those who taste the bliss [of the hereafter]. If you depart from the states of the righteous, you will most surely be among those detained in the horrors of the day of judgment. So, give careful thought—woe be to you—to what you have heard.

If you claim to be as good as the excellent predecessors—satisfied with little, refraining even from what is permitted to you, freely giving of your possessions, preferring others over yourself, unafraid of poverty, hoarding nothing for the morrow, abhorring the amassment of riches, content with poverty and hardship, and delighted with scarcity and a humble station, happy to suffer humiliation and 242
debasement, averse to grandeur and high status, determined and resolute, with a heart that never swerves from right guidance, having called yourself to account before God and brought all your affairs into perfect alignment with what pleases Him, certain that you will not be questioned before the Throne and that, like the righteous and God-fearing, you will not be subjected to a difficult reckoning, since you acquire only lawful wealth to spend it in the cause of God—then woe to you, O misled soul! Give careful thought to the matter, and consider it well. Do you not know that not busying yourself with wealth, and freeing your heart

27 Trans.: The Companions of the Right (see Q. 56:27) are believers who, on the day of resurrection, will receive their record of deeds in their right hand and who, thanks to their faith, will be granted an easy reckoning before God.

[from this preoccupation] for the remembrance of God, contemplation, reflection, and consideration will be better for your *dīn*, ensuring you an easier accounting before God and a gentler questioning, protecting you from the dismays of the day of resurrection, promising you a more bountiful reward, and elevating your standing before God سُبْحَانَهُ وَتَعَالَىٰ many times over?!

We have heard that a certain Companion said, "If one man has a lapful of dinars to give away, while another is engaging in the remembrance of God سُبْحَانَهُ وَتَعَالَىٰ, the one remembering God will be the better of the two."[28]

A certain person of knowledge was once asked about people who amass wealth in order to perform good works, and he said, "It would be more righteous for them to leave [the wealth] untouched."[29]

A certain righteous Successor was once asked about two men, one of whom strove for lawful gain in [this] world, and achieved it, after which he used the money to help his kinfolk and thus stored up reward for himself, while the other avoided accumulating any money at all. He neither sought it out, nor did he spend it [on others]. So, which of the two
243 was better? And [the Successor] replied, "By God, a great distance is between them—as vast as the chasm between the Eastern [provinces of the earth] and the Western—and one side is by far better."

Woe to you! This grace awaits you by abstaining from [this] world, rather than the one who seeks it out. Bear in mind also that in the short term, leaving off your preoccupation with money will be more wholesome for your body, and less tiring, more easeful for your daily living by giving you a clearer conscience and causing you fewer worries. So, what excuse do you have for amassing wealth given the fact that by leaving wealth alone, you will be better off than

28 Narrated by Abū Nuʿaym in *al-Ḥilya* (2:33) on the authority of Abū Baraza al-Aslamī رَضِيَ ٱللَّهُ عَنْهُ.

29 Al-Ḥāfiẓ al-Zabīdī stated in his *Itḥāf* (8:224), "It was narrated by the author of *al-Qūt* on the authority of al-Ḥasan."

someone who has sought out wealth, [even if their purpose is] to spend it in doing righteous works?

Yes, and occupying yourself with the remembrance of God is better than spending money in the cause of God, since [in so doing], you combine peace of mind in this life with well-being and grace in the next.

Furthermore, even if there were great virtue in amassing wealth, you would be bound by the dictates of noble character to emulate your Prophet ﷺ, knowing that God has guided you through him, and to be satisfied with what he chose for himself, namely, to avoid [this] world.

Woe to you! Reflect on what you have heard, and rest assured that happiness and victory lie in the avoidance of [this] world. March in the company of the Chosen One ﷺ, making your way with haste to the garden of refuge. For the Messenger of God ﷺ said, "The foremost believers in the [heavenly] garden are those who, if they had lunch, found no supper; who, if they asked to borrow money, received no loan; who only owned enough clothing to conceal their nakedness; who were unable to acquire that which would make them rich and who, nevertheless, retired at night and rose in the morning content with their Lord. *And whoever obeys God and the Messenger - those will be with the ones upon whom God has bestowed the favor of the prophets, the steadfast affirmers of* 244
truth, the martyrs and the righteous. And excellent are those as companions [Q. 4:69]."[30]

Indeed, my brother, now that you have read this explanation, whenever you amass wealth thenceforth, you will have no basis for your claim that you do so for the purpose of righteousness and acquiring virtue. No, rather, it is out of fear of poverty that you amass [wealth], and for [enjoyment of] worldly comforts, earthly adornments, increase itself, boasting, earthly status, impressing others, making a name

30 Narrated by Abū Nuʿaym in *al-Ḥilya* (7:99) as part of a lengthy *ḥadīth* on the authority of Abū Hurayra.

for yourself, and power and prestige. Yet you claim that it is in order to do good works that you amass wealth!

Woe to you! Be conscious of God, and be ashamed of your pretensions, you mis-led soul!

Woe to you! If you are dazzled by the love of wealth and [this] world, acknowledge that goodness and virtue lie in being content with the bare necessities and shunning excess.

Yes! And when you amass wealth, berate yourself and confess your transgression, fearful of the reckoning [that awaits you]. For this will be more conducive to your salvation and closer to virtue than seeking to justify such amassment of wealth.

My brethren: Know that, in the age of the Companions, there were avenues of lawful gain. Nevertheless, they were among the most scrupulous of all people and the most abstemious, even with regard to the permissible but neutral things (*al-mubāḥ*). As for us, who live in an age in which there is no way to earn one's keep in a lawful fashion, it is difficult to see how we can lawfully earn enough to feed and clothe ourselves. As for amassing wealth in our day, God protect both us and you from that!

So, where else is there any example for us like that of the God-consciousness and scrupulousness of the Companions, any example like their abstention and caution? Where is there any example for us like that of their conscientiousness and purity of intention? By the Lord of the heavens, we
245 have been overcome by the maladies and passions of the soul. The coming of death is close upon us. On the day of resurrection, those who have kept their loads light will be blessed with great happiness, while prolonged sorrow awaits the people of accumulation and delirium. This is the guidance I have offered to you should you accept it, though those who accept it are few. May God in His mercy lead us and you into all goodness.

***

These were the last things he [al-Muḥāsibī] had to say, and they will suffice to demonstrate the superiority of poverty over affluence. Hence, there is no more to add, as evidenced by the fact that [these points] are supported by all the reports we cite in *The Book on the Censure of* [*This*] *World* and *The Book on Poverty and Abstinence.*

[These points] are likewise supported by the following account passed down on the authority of Abū Umāma al-Bāhilī, who said:

> Thaʿlaba b. Ḥāṭib once said, "O Messenger of God, ask God to grant me wealth."
>
> He replied, "O Thaʿlaba, a little for which you give thanks is better than a great deal which is more than you can bear."
>
> He [Thaʿlaba] then said again, "O Messenger of God, ask God to grant me wealth."
>
> "O Thaʿlaba," he asked, "do you not have an exemplar in me? Are you not content to be like the Prophet of God? By the One who holds my soul in His hand, I tell you: If I wanted the mountains to turn to gold and silver for me, they would do so."
>
> "By the One who sent you in truth," [Thaʿlaba replied], "if you ask God to grant me wealth, I will most surely give everyone his due, and I will most surely do this, and do that."
>
> So the Messenger of God صَلَّى ٱللَّهُ عَلَيْهِ وَسَلَّمَ said, "O God, grant wealth to Thaʿlaba."
>
> He [Thaʿlaba] then obtained sheep and goats which multiplied so proliferously that there was no longer room for him in the city [of Medina], so he went elsewhere. After making his home in a valley, he began praying the noon and mid-afternoon prayers communally, and neglecting all the others. As his sheep and goats continued to multiply, he moved still farther from the city, and stopped praying any communal prayers except for the Friday prayer. When his herds went on growing and growing, he stopped attending even the Friday prayer. Instead he would encounter traveling 246
> parties passing by on Fridays and ask them about news from the city.
>
> The Messenger of God صَلَّى ٱللَّهُ عَلَيْهِ وَسَلَّمَ began asking about him, saying, "What has Thaʿlaba b. Ḥāṭib done?"

He was told, "O Messenger of God, he obtained sheep and goats, and there was no longer enough room for him in the city." And he was told all about him.

And he said, "Woe to Thaʿlaba! Woe to Thaʿlaba! Woe to Thaʿlaba!"

Then God سُبْحَانَهُ وَتَعَالَىٰ revealed the words, *Take,* [*O Muḥammad*], *from their wealth a charity by which you purify them and cause them increase, and invoke* [*God's blessings*] *upon them. Indeed, your invocations are reassurance for them.* [Q. 9:103]. God سُبْحَانَهُ وَتَعَالَىٰ thus revealed the religious duties associated with charity (*ṣadaqa*), whereupon the Messenger of God صَلَّى ٱللَّٰهُ عَلَيْهِ وَسَلَّمَ sent two men—one from the tribe of Juhayna and the other from the tribe of Banū Sulaym—to collect the charity that was due, writing them a letter instructing them to collect the charity [from owners of livestock].[31] He instructed the two men to go out and collect the required charity from the Muslims, saying, "Pass by to see Thaʿlaba b. Ḥāṭib and so-and-so (a man from the tribe of Banū Sulaym), and collect the charity they owe."

So the two men went out and asked Thaʿlaba for the charity he owed, reading to him the letter that had been sent by the Messenger of God صَلَّى ٱللَّٰهُ عَلَيْهِ وَسَلَّمَ. In reply, Thaʿlaba said, "This is nothing but a *jizya*, or something akin to it.[32] So be on your way, and when you've finished, come back to me."

So they went to see the man from the tribe of Banū Sulaym. When he heard the two men were coming, he went to get the best of his young camels to offer them as charity. When the two men arrived, he received them and presented them with the camels.

When they saw him, they said, "This is not required of you. We do not wish to take them from you."[33]

"No, take them," the man said.

---

31 It was a document in which he explained [that the charity would consist of] their best young camels, goats and sheep. See *Itḥāf* (8:225).

32 Trans.: By likening the *zakāt* to the *jizya* imposed on non-Muslim subjects of an Islamic state, Thaʿlaba is implying that it is a tax collected against people's will.

33 Trans.: In other words, the man wasn't required to choose the very best of his camels to give away as *zakāt*, and they did not want to take his best camels from him.

When the two men had finished collecting the charity, they passed by Thaʿlaba again and asked him for the charity [he owed].

"Show me your letter," he said. Then he looked at the 247
letter and said, "This is no different from the *jizya*. Be on your way until I decide what to do."

So they set out again and went back to the Messenger of God صَلَّى ٱللَّهُ عَلَيْهِ وَسَلَّمَ. When he saw them, he said, "Woe to Thaʿlaba!" even before they had said a word to him. However, he prayed for blessings upon the man from the tribe of Banū Sulaym. The two men informed him of what Thaʿlaba and the man from Banū Sulaym had done, whereupon God سُبْحَانَهُ وَتَعَالَىٰ revealed the following words concerning Thaʿlaba: *And among them are those who made a covenant with God,* [*saying*], *"If He should give us from His bounty, we will surely spend in charity, and we will surely be among the righteous. But when He gave them from His bounty, they were miserly* (*bakhilū*) *with it and turned away while they refused. So He penalized them with hypocrisy in their hearts until the Day they will meet Him - because they failed God in what they promised Him and because they* [*habitually*] *used to lie* [Q. 9:75-77]. When the Messenger of God صَلَّى ٱللَّهُ عَلَيْهِ وَسَلَّمَ recited what had been revealed concerning Thaʿlaba, he was overheard by one of Thaʿlaba's relatives, who went out until he found Thaʿlaba, and said, "You should be ashamed of yourself, Thaʿlaba. God has revealed such-and-such concerning you."

Thaʿlaba went straightaway to the Prophet صَلَّى ٱللَّهُ عَلَيْهِ وَسَلَّمَ and asked him to receive his charity from him. But he refused, saying, "God has forbidden me to accept your charity from you."

[In distress], he [Thaʿlaba] began strewing dust on his head. The Messenger of God صَلَّى ٱللَّهُ عَلَيْهِ وَسَلَّمَ said to him, "This is your own doing. I commanded you [to give me your charity earlier], and you disobeyed me."

When he continued to refuse to receive anything from him, he [Thaʿlaba] returned home.

When the Messenger of God ﷺ died, Thaʿlaba brought the charity to Abū Bakr the Righteous رَضِيَ ٱللَّهُ عَنْهُ, who likewise refused to receive it from him. Thereafter he took it to ʿUmar b. al-Khaṭṭāb رَضِيَ ٱللَّهُ عَنْهُ, who also refused to receive it.

Thaʿlaba died after the caliphate of ʿUmar b. al-Khaṭṭāb رَضِيَ ٱللَّهُ عَنْهُ.[34]

248 This is the tyranny of wealth and its sinister nature, as you can see from this *ḥadīth*.

Given the blessing of poverty and the curse of affluence, the Messenger of God ﷺ preferred poverty both for himself and the members of his household. About this, it is related that ʿImrān b. Ḥuṣayn رَضِيَ ٱللَّهُ عَنْهُ said:

> I was held in high regard by the Messenger of God ﷺ, who said to me, "ʿImrān, we hold you in high regard. Might you pay a visit to Fāṭima, daughter of the Messenger of God ﷺ?"
>
> "Yes, O Messenger of God," I said, "precious to me as my father and my mother."
>
> So he rose, and I rose with him. When we reached Fāṭima's house رَضِيَ ٱللَّهُ عَنْهَا, he stood at the door and knocked, saying, "Peace be upon you. May I come in?"
>
> "Yes, come in, O Messenger of God," she said.
>
> "And the person who is with me?" he said.
>
> "Who is with you, O Messenger of God?" she asked.
>
> He said, "It is ʿImrān b. Ḥuṣayn."
>
> "By the One who sent you as a prophet," she replied, "I have nothing on but an abaya."
>
> He said, "Do this-and-this with it," gesturing with his hands.
>
> Then she said, "I've covered my body now, but what about my head?"

---

34 Narrated by al-Ṭabarī in his *Tafsīr* (6:10:236), by al-Ṭabarānī in *al-Kabīr* (8:218), by Abū Nuʿaym in *Maʿrifat al-Ṣaḥāba* [Knowing the Companions] (1:495), and by al-Bayhaqī in *al-Shuʿab* (4048). His statement that "Thaʿlaba died after the caliphate of ʿUmar b. al-Khaṭṭāb" indicates that he died during the caliphate of ʿUthmān رَضِيَ ٱللَّهُ عَنْهُ, as is stated explicitly by the other narrators.

> He then tossed her a threadbare wrap he had been wearing, saying, "Secure it around your head."
>
> Then she permitted him to enter, and he said, "Peace be upon you, my daughter. How are you this morning?"
>
> "Actually," she said, "I woke up in pain. And the pain is made worse by the fact that I have nothing to eat. The hunger is exhausting me."
>
> Weeping, the Messenger of God صلى الله عليه وسلم said, "Do 249
> not be distressed, my daughter. For God is my witness, I have not tasted food for three days, and this despite the fact that I have a higher station before God than you do. If I asked my Lord, He would feed me. However, I have preferred the hereafter over [this] world."
>
> Patting her on the shoulder, he added, "Rejoice. For God is my witness: You are the foremost of the women of the garden."
>
> "So what status is occupied by Āsiya, wife of Pharaoh,[35] and Maryam the daughter of ʿImrān?"
>
> He replied, "Āsiya is the foremost of women in her world, Maryam is the foremost of women in her world, Khadīja is the foremost of women in her world, and you are the foremost of women in your world. You shall dwell in houses of gold and silver brocade in which no harmful word or clamor shall be heard."
>
> Then he said to her, "Be content with your paternal cousin. For truly I tell you, I have given you in marriage to one who is foremost among men both in [this] world and the hereafter."[36]

Think now about the condition of Faṭima, the Messenger of God's صلى الله عليه وسلم flesh and blood, and how she preferred poverty and abandoned wealth.

---

35 Trans.: Āsiya bt. Muzāḥim is the name assigned in Muslim tradition to the wife of the Pharaoh in the time of Moses who, after Moses' mother had cast the child into the water at God's command, rescued the infant from the river, then took him into her care while allowing his mother to nurse him. See Q. 20:36-39, 28:7-13 and 66:11.

36 Narrated by al-Ājurrī in *al-Sharīʿa* (1607); by Aḥmad in his *Musnad* (5:26) in an abbreviated form from a ḥadīth of Maʿqil b. Yasār رضي الله عنه, by al-Ṭabarānī in *al-Kabīr* (20:229), and by Ibn ʿAsākir in *Tārīkh Dimashq* (42:126).

Whoever heeds the states of the prophets and saints, their words, and the reports passed down of the things they did, will have no doubt that the lack of wealth is better than its presence, even if it is spent on good deeds. For even if someone is performing his duties, giving others their due, not putting it to dubious uses, and spending on good deeds, it will still cause him to be preoccupied with taking care of it and distract him from the remembrance of God, since there can be no remembrance of God unless he is free of distractions, and no one can be free of distractions if he is busy thinking about wealth.

The following story was told by Jarīr, who heard it from al-Layth:

250 A certain man said to Jesus son of Mary عَلَيْهِ ٱلسَّلَامُ, "I would like to be with you and accompany you."

So the two of them set off. After some time they came to a riverbank, where they sat down and ate lunch. They had three loaves of bread of which they ate two, so one was left. Jesus عَلَيْهِ ٱلسَّلَامُ got up, went down to the river and drank. When he returned, he did not find the third loaf of bread, so he asked the man, "Who took the other loaf of bread?"

"I don't know," he said.

So [Jesus] set off with his companion. After some time, he saw a female gazelle, and with her were two does. He called to one of the two does, and it came to him. He then slaughtered it and roasted some of it, and he and the man ate.

Then he said to the doe, "Rise, by God's permission." So it rose and went away.

Turning to the man, Jesus said, "By the One who showed you this sign, tell me: Who took the other loaf?"

"I don't know," he said.

They then came to a *wadi* filled with water. Jesus took the man's hand and the two of them walked on the water. When they had crossed, he said again, "By the One who showed you this sign, tell me: Who took the other loaf?"

"I don't know," he replied.

They then came to a desert, and sat down. As they sat there, Jesus عَلَيْهِ ٱلسَّلَامُ took some dust or sand and said, "By the permission of God سُبْحَانَهُ وَتَعَالَى, be gold," whereupon it turned to gold. Dividing the gold into thirds, he said, "A third is for me, a third is for you, and a third is for whoever it was that took the other loaf."

"I am the one who took the other loaf," [the man] said.

"It's all yours," he عَلَيْهِ السَّلَامُ replied, and departed.

Two men then came along and found [this man] in the desert with the money, and wanted to take it and kill him.

"We'll divide it among the three of us," he said. "Send somebody to the village to buy us something to eat."

So, they sent one of them. The one who had been sent to the village then said, "Why should I share this money with the others? I'll poison the food and kill both of them. Then I'll take the money for myself."

So, he determined to do it. Meanwhile, the two men who 251
had sent him said, "Why should we let this person have a third of the money? When he gets back, we'll kill him and divide the money between us."

When the man came back, the two others killed him, and then ate the food and died. Thus, the money remained in the desert, with the three men murdered beside it.

Passing by them, Jesus عَلَيْهِ السَّلَامُ said to his companions about the situation, "[What you see] is [this] world—beware of it."[37]

It is said that Dhū l-Qarnayn[38] came upon a community of people who owned none of the worldly goods people [generally] enjoy. These people had dug graves which, when they awoke in the morning, they would sweep and otherwise maintain. They also prayed at the graves. They grazed on plants like animals, as they had been foreordained to live off the plants of the earth.

---

37 Narrated by Ibn Abī al-Dunyā in *al-Zuhd* (177), and by Ibn ʿAsākir in *Tārīkh Dimashq* (47:394).

38 Trans.: Dhū l-Qarnayn is a figure referred to in Q. 18:83-101. He has been identified inconclusively with a variety of historical figures, including Alexander the Great, Chosroes, Cyrus the Great, and others.

Dhū l-Qarnayn sent for their ruler, saying, "Answer Dhū l-Qarnayn."

[The ruler] said, "I have no need of him. If he has some need, let him come to me."

[Hearing what the ruler had said,] Dhū l-Qarnayn said, "He has spoken truly."

He thereupon went to see the ruler and said to him, "I sent for you, but you refused to come. So I have come to you."

The ruler replied, "If I had need of you, I would have come to you."

Dhū l-Qarnayn then asked, "Why do I see you in a condition in which I have never seen any other nation?"

"What [condition] is that?" the ruler asked.

"You have nothing of [this] world," Dhū l-Qarnayn said. "Why don't you take gold and silver and enjoy them?"

[The people] said, "We abhor them, because those who acquire either of them develop a craving for them and want something better."

"So why have you dug graves?" asked [Dhū l-Qarnayn]. "Why do you take care of them after you rise in the morning?
252 And why do you sweep them and pray at them?"

They said, "When we look at them, we want the graves to keep us from placing our hope in [this] world."

He continued, "I also see that you have no food but green plants that come from the earth. Why don't you take livestock and milk them, ride them, and enjoy them?"

And they replied, "We hate to make our bellies into graves for them. Besides, we have all we need in the plants of the earth. The minimum amount of food is enough for people to live on. Nothing that crosses our palates has any taste to us, no matter what kind of food it is."

Then the ruler of that territory reached out behind Dhū l-Qarnayn and picked up a skull. "O Dhū l-Qarnayn," he asked, "Do you know who this is?"

"No," he replied. "Who is it?"

"It belonged to a king to whom God had given power over the people of the land, and who was brutal, unjust, and tyrannical. When God سُبْحَانَهُ وَتَعَالَىٰ saw how this king had comported himself, he struck him dead, causing him to become like a mere rock cast to the ground. God had counted his actions against him, to recompense him for them in the hereafter."

Then he picked up another worn skull. "O Dhū l-Qarnayn," he asked, "Do you know who this is?"

"No," he replied. "Who is it?"

He said, "It belonged to a king to whom God granted sovereignty thereafter. Having seen the brutality, injustice, and tyranny of his predecessor, this king feared God عَزَّ وَجَلَّ, humbled himself, and commanded that justice be done for the inhabitants of his realm. Then he became as you can see. God has counted his actions against him, to recompense him for them in the hereafter."

Then he reached out for Dhū l-Qarnayn's skull, and said, "And this skull—it's as though it had become like those other two. Look at what you do, O Dhū l-Qarnayn."

To this Dhū l-Qarnayn replied, "Can you accompany me, and allow me to adopt you as a brother, a minister, and a partner in the wealth God has given me?"

And the king said, "It would not be good for me or my people to be in the same place with you."

"And why is that?" asked Dhū l-Qarnayn.

"Because all people are your enemies, whereas they are 253
friends of mine."

"And why is that?" he asked again.

"They feel enmity toward you because of the power, wealth, and [the advantages of this] world that you possess, whereas no one feels enmity toward me since I have rejected these things but, instead, I experience scarcity and need."

At this, Dhū l-Qarnayn took his leave [of the king], astonished and humbled by him.[39]

***

39 Narrated by Abū al-Shaykh in *al-ʿAẓama* (958), and by Ibn al-Jawzī in *al-Muntaẓam* (1:185), where he took it from the chain of narrators relied upon by Ibn Abī al-Dunyā.

These stories, together with what we have presented before, will show you the harms of affluence (*āfāt al-ghinā*). And God is the One who leads the way to what is right.

***

The Book on the Censure of Wealth and Miserliness,
being the seventh book of the Quarter of Perils
of *The Revival of the Religious Sciences,*
is herewith completed
with praise to God for His gracious assistance,
to be followed by
The Book on The Censure of Fame and Ostentation.

***

Bibliography

ʿAbd al-Razzāq b. Hammām al-Ṣanʿānī. *al-Muṣannaf*. Ed. Ḥabīb al-Raḥmān al-ʿAẓamī. Beirut: Maktab al-Islāmī, 1983.

al-Abshīhī, Manṣūr. *al-Mustaṭraf min kullī fannin mustaẓraf*. First Edition. Ed. Mufīd Qamīḥa. Lebanon: Dār al-Kutub al-ʿIlmiyya, 1983.

Abū ʿAbd al-Raḥmān al-Sulamī. *Ādāb al-Ṣuḥba*. Ed. Majdī Fatḥī al-Sayyid. First Edition. Egypt: Dār al-Ṣaḥāba li-l-Turāth, 1999.

Abū al-ʿAtāhiya. *Ashʿāruhu wa Akhbāruhu li-l-Shāʿir al-Mubdiʿ al-Muwallid Ismāʿīl b. al-Qāsim b. Suwayd al-Maʿrūf bi Abī al-ʿAtāhiya* (d. 211/826). Ed. Shukrī Fayṣal, First Edition. Syria: Dār al-Mallāḥ, 1964.

Abū al-Baqā' al-ʿUkbarī. *Sharḥ Dīwān al-Mutanabbī*. Final Edition. Egypt: Maktaba wa Maṭbaʿat Muṣṭafā al-Bābī al-Ḥalabī, 1971.

Abū Dāwūd, Sulaymān b. al-Ashʿath al-Sijistānī. *Sunan Abī Dāwūd*. Ed. ʿIzzat ʿAbīd al-Daʿʿās and ʿĀdil al-Sayyid. Beirut: Dār Ibn Ḥazm, 1997.

Abū Manṣūr al-Thaʿālibī. *al-Tamthīl wa-l-Muḥāḍara*. Ed. ʿAbd al-Fattāḥ Muḥammad al-Ḥilw. Second Edition. Egypt: al-Dār al-ʿArabiya li-l-Kitāb, 1983.

Abū Nuʿaym al-Iṣbahānī, Aḥmad b. ʿAbdallāh. *Ḥilyat al-Awliyāʾ wa-Ṭabaqāt al-Aṣfiyāʾ*. Cairo: Maṭbaʿat al-Saʿāda wa-l-Khānijī, 1357/1938. Beirut: Dār al-Kitāb al-ʿArabī, 1987.

———. *Tārīkh Iṣbahān*. Ed. Sayyid Kusrawī Ḥasan. Beirut: Dār al-Kutub al-ʿIlmiyya, 1990.

Abū al-Shaykh, ʿAbdullāh b. Muḥammad b. Jaʿfar b. Ḥayyān. *al-ʿAẓama*. Ed. Riḍā Allāh b. Muḥammad al-Mubārakfūrī. Second Edition. Saudi Arabia: Dār al-ʿĀṣima, 1998.

———. *Ṭabaqāt al-Muḥaddithīn*. Ed. ʿAbd al-Ghafūr al-Balūshī. Beirut: Muʾassassat al-Risāla, 1992.

———. *al-Tawbīkh wa-l-Tanbīh*. Ed. Ḥasan b. Amīn al-Danwa. Egypt: Maktabat al-Tawʿiya al-Islāmiya, 1408/1988.

Abū Ṭālib al-Makkī, Muḥammad b. ʿAlī. *Qūt al-qulūb*. Ed. Muḥammad al-Zaharī al-Ghumurāwī. Cairo: al-Maṭbaʿat al-Maymaniyya, 1310/1893. Beirut: Dār Ṣādir/Dār al-Fikr, n.d.

Abū Yaʿlā, Aḥmad b. ʿAlī. *Musnad Abī Yaʿlā l-Mawṣūlī*. Ed. Ḥusayn Salīm Asad al-Dārānī. Damascus: Dār al-Maʾmūn li-l-Turāth and Dār al-Thaqafa al-ʿArabiyya, 1989.

al-Ājurrī, Muḥammad b. al-Ḥusayn. *al-Sharīʿa*. First Edition. Lebanon: Mu'assasat al-Rayyān, 2008.

Alī b. Abī Ṭālib. *Anwār al-ʿUqūl li-Waṣī al-Rasūl*. Ed. ʿAbd al-Majīd Hamū. Beirut: Dār Ṣādir, 2010.

al-ʿAskarī, Ismāʿīl. *Taṣḥīfāt al-Muḥaddithīn*. First Edition. Egypt: al-Maṭbaʿa al-ʿArabiyya al-Ḥadīth, 1983.

al-Azraqī, Muḥammad b. ʿAbdallāh b. Aḥmad. *Akhbār Makka wa-mā Jaʾa fīhā min al-Āthār*. Ed. ʿAlī ʿUmar. Cairo: Makatabat al-Thaqāfa al-Dīniyya, 2004.

al-Bayhaqī, Aḥmad b. al-Ḥusayn. *Shuʿab al-Īmān*. Ed. Muḥammad al-Saʿīd b. Basyūnī Zaghlūl. Beirut: Dār al-Kutub al-ʿIlmiyyya, 2000.

———. *Shuʿab al-Īmān*. Beirut: Dār al-Kutub al-ʿIlmiyya, 1410/1990.

———. *al-Jāmiʿ li-Shuʿab al-Īmān*. Ed. ʿAbd al-ʿAlī ʿAbd al-Ḥamīd Ḥamid. Riyadh: Maktabat al-Rushd. 2004.

———. *Manāqib al-Shāfiʿī*. Ed. Aḥmad Ṣaqr. Cairo: Maktabat Dār al-Turāth, 1971.

———. *al-Zuhd al-Kabīr*. Third Edition. Ed. Sheikh ʿĀmir Aḥmad Ḥaydar. Lebanon: Mu'assasat al-Kutub al-Thaqāfiyya, 1996.

al-Bukhārī, Muḥammad b. Ismāʿīl. *al-Adab al-Mufrad*. Ed. Muḥammad Fūʾād ʿAbd al-Bāqī. Cairo: al-Maktab al-Salafiyya, 1997.

———. *Ṣaḥīḥ al-Bukhārī*. Būlāq, 1311–13; repr. Beirut: Dār Ṭawq al-Najāt, 1422/2001.

al-Bazzār, Abū Bakr b. Aḥmad b. ʿAmr. *al-Baḥr al-Zakhkhār* (known as *Musnad al-Bazzār*). Ed. Maḥfūẓ al-Raḥmān Zayn Allāh. Medina: Maktabat al-ʿUlūm wa-l-Ḥikam, 1988.

al-Dāraquṭnī, ʿAlī b. ʿUmar. *Sunan al-Dāraquṭnī*. Ed. ʿAbdallāh Hashim Yamānī. Beirut: Dār al-Maʿrifa, 1966 [repr.].

———. *al-ʿIlal al-Wārida fī al-Aḥādīth al-Nabawiyya*. Ed. Maḥfūẓ al-Raḥmān Zayn Allāh and Muḥammad Ṣāliḥ al-Dabāsī. Saudi Arabia: Dār Ṭayba and Dār Ibn al-Jawzī, 2003.

al-Daylamī, Shīrawayh b. Shahdār. *al-Firdaws bi-Maʾthūr al-Khiṭāb = Musnad al-Firdaws*. Ed. Saʿīd b. Basyūnī Zaghlūl. Beirut: Dār al-Kutub al-ʿIlmiyya, 1986.

al-Dhahabī, Muḥammad b. Aḥmad. *Siyar Aʿlām al-Nubalāʾ*. Ed. Shuʿayb al-Arnāʾūṭ, et al. Beirut: Muʾassasat al-Risāla, 1996.

al-Dīnawarī, Aḥmad b. Marwān b. Muḥammad. *al-Mujālasa wa-Jawāhir al-ʿIlm*. Beirut: Dār Ibn Ḥazm, 2002.

al-Fāhikī, Muḥammad b. Isḥāq al-ʿAbbās. *Akhbār Makka fī Qadīm al-Dahr wa-l-Ḥadīth*. Ed. ʿAbd al-Malik ʿAbdallāh Dahayyash. Beirut: Dār Khiḍr, 1414.

al-Ḥākim al-Nīsābūrī, Muḥammad b. ʿAbdallāh. *al-Mustadrak ʿalā al-Ṣaḥiḥayn*. Hyderabad: Dāʾirat al-Maʿārif al-Niẓāmiyya, 1335/1917 [repr. Beirut: Dār al-Maʿrifa, n.d.].

al-Ḥakīm al-Tirmidhī, Muḥammad b. ʿAlī. *Khatam al-Awliyāʾ*. Ed. ʿUthmān Ismāʾīl Yaḥyā. Beirut: al-Maṭbaʿ al-Kāthūlīkīyya, 1965.

———. *Nawādir al-Uṣūl*. Beirut: Dār Ṣādir, n.d. [reprint Cairo, 1293/1876 edition].

———. *Sunan al-Tirmidhī = al-Jāmiʿ al-Ṣaḥīḥ*. Ed. Aḥmad Shākir, Muḥammad Fuʾād ʿAbd al-Bāqī, and Ibrāhīm ʿAṭwa. Beirut: Dār Iḥyāʾ al-Turāth al-ʿArabī, n.d. [reprint of Cairo, 1938 edition].

al-Ḥamawī, Yaqūt. *Muʿjam al-Udabāʾ*. First Edition. Introduced by ʿUmar Fārūq al-Ṭibāʿ. Lebanon: Mu'assasat al-Maʿārif, 1999.

Hannād. *al-Zuhd*. First Edition. Ed. ʿAbd al-Raḥmān b. ʿAbd al-Jabbār al-Farwā'ī. Kuwait: Dār al-Khulafā' li-l-Kitāb al-Islāmī, 1406/1986.

Ibn ʿAbd al-Barr, Yūsuf b. ʿAbdallāh. *Bahjat al-Majālis*. Ed. Muḥammad Mursī al-Khūrī. Beirut: Dār alKutub al-ʿIlmiyya, 1981.

———. *al-Intiqāʾ fī faḍāʾil al-Thalāthat al-Aʾimmat al-Fuqahāʾ*. Ed. ʿAbd al-Fattāḥ Abū Ghudda. Beirut: Dār al-Bashāʾir al-Islāmiyya, 1997.

———. *al-Tamhīd*. Casablanca: Wizārat al-Awqāf, 1967.

Ibn ʿAbd Rabbihi, Aḥmad b. Muḥammad al-Andalūsī. *al-ʿIqd al-farīd*. Ed. Aḥmad al-Amīn, Aḥmad al-Zayn, and Ibrāhīm al-Ibārī. Cairo: Lajnat al-Taʾlīf wa-Tarjama wa-Nashr, 1940.

Ibn Abī al-Dunyā, ʿAbdallāh b. Muḥammad al-Qurashī. *Dhamm al-Dunyā*. Ed. Muḥammad ʿAbd al-Qādir Aḥmad ʿAṭā. Beirut: Muʾassasat al-Kutub al-Thaqafiyya, 1993.

———. *al-Faraj baʿd al-Shidda*. First Edition. Ed. Muṣṭafā. ʿAbd al-Qādir Aḥmad ʿAṭā. Lebanon: Mu'assasat al-Kutub al-Thaqāfiyya, 1993.

———. *al-Ḥilm*. Ed. Majdī al-Sayyid Ibrāhīm. Egypt: Maktabat al-Qur'ān, n.d.

———. *al-Ikhwān*. Ed. Muṣṭafā ʿAbd al-Qādir ʿAṭā. First Edition. Lebanon: Dār al-Kutub al-ʿIlmiyya, 1988.

———. *Iṣlāḥ al-Māl*. Ed. Muḥammad ʿAbd al-Qādir ʿAṭā. Beirut: Muʾssassat al-Kutub al-Thaqafiyya, 1993.

———. *Kitāb al-Awliyā*. Ed. Muḥammad al-Saʿīd b. Basyūnī Zaghlūl. First Edition. Lebanon: Mu'assasat al-Kutub al-Thaqāfiyya, 1993.

———. *Makārim al-akhlāq*. Ed. Majdī al-Sayyid Ibrāhīm. Cairo: Maktabat al-Qurʾān, n.d.

———. *Mudārāt al-Nās*. First Edition. Ed. Muḥammad Khayr Ramaḍān Yūsuf. Lebanon: Dār Ibn Ḥazm, 1998.

———. *Qaḍā' al-Ḥawā'ij*. First Edition. Ed. Muḥammad ʿAbd al-Qādir Aḥmad ʿAṭā. Lebanon: Mu'assasat al-Kutub al-Thaqāfiyya, 1993.

———. *al-Ṣamt wa-Ādāb al-Lisān*. Ed. Najm ʿAbd al-Raḥmān Khalaf. Beirut: Dār al-Gharb al-Islāmī, 1986.

———. *al-Yaqīn*. Ed. Yāsīn Muḥammad al-Sawās. Beirut: Dār al-Bashāʾir al-Islāmiyya, 2004.

———. *al-Zuhd*. First Edition. Syria: Dār Ibn Kathīr, 1999.

Ibn Abī al-Ḥadīd. *Sharḥ Nahj al-Balāgha*. Ed. Muḥammad Abū al-Faḍl Ibrāhīm. Egypt: Dār Iḥyāʾ al-Kutub al-ʿArabiyya, n.d.

Ibn Abī Shayba, ʿAbdallāh b. Muḥammad. *al-Muṣannaf*. Ed. Muḥammad ʿAwāmma. Jedda: Dār al-Minhāj, 2006.

Ibn ʿAdī = ʿAbdallāh b. ʿAdī al-Jurjānī. *al-Kāmil fī Ḍuʿafāʾ al-Rijāl*. Ed. Suhayl Zakkār and Yaḥyā Mukhtār Ghazāwī. Beirut: Dār al-Fikr, 1988.

Ibn ʿAsākir, ʿAlī b. al-Ḥasan. *Tārīkh Madīnat Dimashq*. Ed. Muḥibb al-Dīn ʿUmar b. Gharāma al-ʿUmrāwī. Beirut: Dār al-Fikr, 1995.

Ibn al-Athīr. *Asad al-Ghāba fī Maʿrifat al-Ṣaḥāba*. Ed. Muḥammad Ibrāhīm al-Bannā, Muḥammad Aḥmad ʿĀshūr and Muḥammad ʿAbd al-Wahhāb Fāyid. First Edition. Egypt: Dār al-Shaʿb, 1970.

Ibn Ḥajar al-ʿAsqalānī. *al-Iṣāba fī Tamyīz al-Ṣaḥāba*. First Edition. Lebanon: Dār al-Kitāb al-ʿArabī, 1359/ 1940.

Ibn Ḥanbal, Aḥmad. *Musnad al-Imām Aḥmad b. Ḥanbal*. Ed. Shuʿayb al-Arnāʾūṭ. Beirut: Muʾassasat al-Risāla, 1995.

———. *al-Zuhd*. Ed. Muḥammad ʿAbd al-Salam Shāhīn. Beirut: Dār al-Kutub al-ʿIlmiyya, 1999.

Ibn Ḥibbān, Abū Hatim Muḥammad al-Tamīmī al-Bustī. *Rawḍat al-ʿUqalāʾ*. Ed. ʿAbd al-ʿAlīm Muḥammad al-Darwīsh. Damascus: al-Hayʾa al-ʿĀmma al-Sūriyya li-l-Kitāb, 2009.

———. *al-Majrūḥīn min al-Muḥaddithīn*. First Edition. Ed. Ḥamdī ʿAbd al-Majīd al-Salafī. Saudi Arabia: Dār al-Ṣumayʿī, 2000.

———. *Ṣaḥīḥ Ibn Ḥibbān = al-Musnad al-Ṣaḥīḥ ʿalā al-Taqāsīm wa-l-Anwāʿ*. Ed. Aḥmad Shākir. Cairo: Dār al-Maʿārif, 1952.

Ibn al-Jawzī. *al-Mudhish*. First Edition. Syria: Dār al-Qalam, 2004.

———. *al-Muntaẓam fī Tawārīkh al-Mulūk wa-l-Umam*. First Edition. Ed. Suhayl Zakkār. Lebanon: Dār al-Fikr, 1995.

Ibn Mājah, Muḥammad b. Yazīd. *Sunan Ibn Mājah*. Ed. Muḥammad Fuʾād ʿAbd al-Bāqī. Cairo: Dār Iḥyāʾ al-Kutub al-ʿArabiyya, 1954.

Ibn Manẓūr. *Mukhtaṣar Tārīkh Dimashq*. First Edition. Syria: Dār al-Fikr, 1984.

Ibn Qutayba al-Dīnawayrī, ʿAbdallāh b. Muslim. *ʿUyūn al-Akhbār*. Cairo: Dār al-Kutub al-Miṣriyya, 1930.

Ibn Saʿd = Muḥammad b. Saʿd al-Baṣrī. *al-Ṭabaqāt al-Kabīr*. Ed. ʿAlī Muḥammad ʿUmar. Cairo: Maktabat al-Khanjī, 2001.

Ibn Zanjawayh. *al-Amwāl*. Ed. Shākir Dhīb Fayyāḍ. First Edition. Saudi Arabia: Markaz al-Malik Fayṣal li-l-Buḥūth wa-l-Dirāsāt al-Islāmiyya, 1986.

al-Kharāʾiṭī. *Iʿtilāl al-Qulūb*. Ed. Ḥamdī al-Darmadāsh. Second Edition. Saudi Arabia: Maktabat Nizār Muṣṭafā al-Bāz, 2000.

al-Khaṭīb al-Baghdādī, Aḥmad b. ʿAlī. *Tārīkh Baghdād*. Ed. Muṣṭafā ʿAbd al-Qādir ʿAṭā. Beirut: Dār al-Kutub al-ʿIlmiyya, 1997.

al-Kharāʾiṭī, Muḥammad b. Jaʿfar. *Masāwiʾ al-Akhlāq*. Ed. Muṣṭafā ʿAṭā. Beirut: Muʾassasat al-Kutub al-Thaqāfiyya, 1993.

al-Muḥāsibī, Ibn Asad. *al-Waṣāyā*. First Edition. Ed. ʿAbd al-Qādir Aḥmad ʿAṭā. Lebanon: Dār al-Kutub al-ʿIlmiyya, 1986.

al-Nasāʾī, Aḥmad b. Shuʿayb. *Sunan al-Nasāʾī*. Cairo: al-Maṭbaʿat al-Maymaniyya, 1312/1894; repr. Beirut: Dār al-Kitāb al-ʿArabī.

al-Qāḍī Iyāḍ. *al-Ilmāʿ*. Ed. al-Sayyid Aḥmad Ṣaqr. Third Edition. Egypt: Maktabat Dār al-Turāth, 2004.

al-Quḍāʿī, Muḥammad b. Salāma. *Musnad al-Shihāb*. Ed. Ḥamdī ʿAbd al-Majīd al-Salafī. Beirut: Muʾassasat al-Risāla, 1985.

al-Qushayrī, ʿAbd al-Karīm. *al-Risāla al-Qushayriyya*. Ed. ʿAbd al-Ḥalīm Maḥmūd and Maḥmūd b. al-Sharīf. Cairo: Dār al-Shaʿab, 1989.

al-Shāfiʿī, Muḥammad b. Idrīs. *Dīwān*. Ed. Yūsuf ʿAlī Badawī. Damascus: Maktabat Dār al-Fajr, 2000.

———. *Musnad al-Imām al-Shāfiʿī*. Ed. Ayyūb Abū Khashrīf. Damascus: Dār al-Thaqāfa al-ʿArabī, 2002.

al-Shāshī, Abū Bakr. *Fawāʾid Abī Bakr al-Shāshī*. First Edition. Ed. Samīr b. Ḥusayn Walad Saʿdī al-Ḥusnī. Saudi Arabia: Maktabat al-Rushd, 1998.

al-Ṭabarānī, Sulaymān b. Aḥmad. *al-Muʿjam al-Awsaṭ*. First Edition. Ed. Maḥmūd al-Ṭaḥḥān. Saudi Arabia: Maktabat al-Maʿārif, 1985.

———. *al-Muʿjam al-Kabīr*. Ed. Ḥamdī ʿAbd al-Majīd al-Salafī. Beirut: Dār Iḥyāʾ al-Turāth al-ʿArabī, n.d.

———. *al-Muʿjam al-Ṣaghīr*. Beirut: Dār al-Kutub al-ʿIlmiyya, 1983 [repr.].

al-Thaʿālibī, ʿAbd al-Malik b. Muḥammad Abū Manṣūr. *al-Tamthīl wa-l-Muḥāḍara*. Second Edition. Ed. ʿAbd al-Fattāḥ Muḥammad al-Ḥilw. Egypt: al-Dār al-ʿArabiyya li-l-Kitāb, 1983.

al-Thaʿlabī, Aḥmad b. Muḥammad. *Tafsīr al-Thaʿlabī = al-Kashf wa-l-Bayān*. Ed. Abū Muḥammad b. ʿĀshūr. Beirut: Dār Iḥyāʾ al-Turāth al-ʿArabī, 2002.

al-Warrāq, Maḥmūd. *Dīwān Maḥmūd al-Warrāq*. Ed. Walīd al-Qaṣṣāb. First Edition. United Arab Emirates. Mu'assasat al-Funūn, 1991.

al-Zabıdı, Muḥammad Murtaḍā. *Itḥāf al-Sāda al-Muttaqīn bi-Sharḥ Iḥyāʾ ʿUlūm al-Dīn*. 10 vols. [Cairo]: al-Maṭbaʿat al-Maymūniyya, 1311/1894.

Index of Qurʾānic Verses

Index of *Ḥadīth*

Index of People and Places

Subject Index

About the Translator

Nancy N. Roberts

Nancy N. Roberts is a translator of Arabic literature. She has received the University of Arkansas Translation Award and a commendation from the judges of the 2008 Banipal Prize. For Fons Vitae she has translated *Islamic Jurisprudence According to the Four Sunni Schools, Volume I: Modes of Islamic Worship* by Abd al-Rahman Ibn Muhammad Awad al-Jaziri, *The Subtle Blessings in the Saintly Lives of Abu al-Abbas al-Mursi and His Master Abu al-Hasan*, by Ibn 'Ata' Allah al-Iskandari, as well as the present work.